THE SILE

Jesus said: 'Let not him who seeks cease until he finds, and when he finds he shall be astonished; astonished he shall reach the Kingdom, and having reached the Kingdom he shall rest.'

(From the *Oxyrhyncus Papyrus* Third Century A.D.)

W. Tudor Pole

THE SILENT ROAD

In the Light of Personal Experience

NEVILLE SPEARMAN
THE C. W. DANIEL COMPANY LTD

© W. TUDOR POLE,
LONDON, 1960

ISBN 85435 443 3
First published 1960
Second impression 1965
Third impression March 1969
Fourth impression November 1972
Fifth impression December 1978
Sixth impression May 1987

Printed in Great Britain by
Hillman Printers (Frome) Ltd., Somerset
for the publishers.

THE CONTENTS

Foreword	page	ix
Introduction		xi

Part I

1	Passers By	3
2	An Account of Three Supernatural Experiences	6
	Love's Victory over Death	7
	A Healing Mission	10
	The Monk of Tintern Abbey	12
3	Further Unusual Incidents	19
	A Puzzling Time Sequence	19
	Transit Most Mysterious	23
	A Ring of Surprise	24
	An Aftermath of Suicide	26
4	Memory, Time and Prevision	30
5	Psychic Methods of Reception	44
	The Dangers of Psychic Automatism	45
	An Observer on the 'Other Side'	46
	Building for the Future	56
	Communion and Communication	57
6	The Enigma of Sex	59
7	The Attitude of the Sceptic	63
	The Closed Mind	66

	THE CONTENTS	
8	SPIRITUAL HEALING	page 73
	Healing 'Miracles'—Abdul Baha	75
	Padre Pio	80
9	THE GENIE AND THE LAMP	83
	The Genie and the Little Horse	85
	The Genie and the Storm	88
10	CONSCIENCE—A HOUND FROM HEAVEN	90
11	SOME SPIRITUAL ISSUES UNDERLYING WORLD PROBLEMS	95

Part II

1	THE MYSTERY OF DREAMS	107
	Premonitions	109
	An Incident at Karnak in Egypt	111
	A Foreign Legionary Meets Himself	111
	A Waking Dream Experience	112
	The Soul in Relation to the Spirit and the Mind	118
2	MOUSSA THE SNAKE-CHARMER	120
3	A PERSONAL NOTE	126
	The Uses of Prevision	128
	'Tell Her to be My Mother'	130
	The Problem of Evidence	131
	The Transience of Existence	132
	An Experience on the Orient Express	133
	A Case of Intervention	134
	The Saving Presence	134
	The Origin of the Silent Minute	138

THE CONTENTS

4	'Voices'	page 141
5	The Problem of Survival	150
	Time and Timelessness	153
6	Seven Facets of the Mind	155
7	The Lure of Ancient Egypt	162
	'For the King's House in the Desert'	162
	The Desert, The Khamsin and The Sphinx	167
8	An Exercise in the Use of the Imagination	172
9	Food for Thought	177
	On Meditation	177
	The Gift of Giving	180
	To One Bereaved	182
	Affluence	187
	Thinking from the Summit	189
10	Light out of Darkness	194
	The Illusion Called Evil	202
11	Times of Tribulation	205
12	A Colloquy Between the Author and His Publisher	210
13	Chalice Well and 'the Upper Room'	221

Foreword

RECOGNITION OF THE *truth or value of the supernormal experiences recorded in this book cannot be communicated by the author to his readers.*
Awareness of reality must inevitably be reached interiorly. For this reason I have no desire to bring conviction to those who may regard what I have written as being incredible or the product of a fertile imagination. It is well, however, to remind ourselves occasionally that in almost every field of research the so-called fantasies of yesterday often become the facts of today. The horizons of the mind are not fixed: they are expanding ceaselessly. Therefore it is suggested that what I have recorded should be read with a mind free from preconceived ideas or set opinions. The search for Truth is a personal and solitary adventure. All we can do is to share ideas with one another, in the hope that by doing so the light of understanding may bring us a little nearer to Reality. In the long run it is through silence, and not through speech, that Revelation is received.

W. T. P.

London, S.W.1.
1960.

Introduction

By The Hon. Brinsley le Poer Trench

SOME PEOPLE ARE publicists; others act unseen behind the scenes and let their deeds speak for themselves. Tudor Pole is one of the latter group. If you passed him in the street you would not realise that there was anything particularly unusual about him. But he is, I assure you, a quite exceptional man.

He is utterly modest and unassuming. Although he would never admit it, I dare say that half his life has been spent in listening to people's troubles and advising them on how to overcome their problems. In addition, I suspect that much of his sleeping life is also taken up with problems concerning the world's affairs. And by this I mean actual spiritual work while he is 'out of the body' in the sleep state.

Tudor Pole is the confidant of the great and the lowly, the rich and the poor. He is a kind of Albert Schweitzer for the sick in mind. And yet he is wise enough to know that nobody can solve another's troubles or run their lives for them. One cannot permit another to take over one's own burdens and liabilities, leaving one, as it were, free and comfortable, without responsibilities. Each one of us has to find his own way and salvation. Spiritual and material progress lies solely with the individual. Outsiders can only point the way. And this is what Tudor Pole, in his wisdom, tells each one who comes seeking solace.

Although he has had many astonishing experiences of a most singular nature, some of which are described in these pages, he has his feet firmly anchored on the ground. The greater part of his life, apart from five years in the Army, has been spent in the world of industry. However, his interests are decidedly varied. He has travelled widely and has undertaken archaeological research in Egypt, Palestine, Turkey and the Sahara.

In 1940, at the time of Dunkirk, he founded the Big Ben Silent Minute. He asked people everywhere to enter at nine each evening into a dedicated silent prayer for Peace. Today, nearly twenty years later, there is hardly a country in the world where this practice is not known and kept. In the words of its founder: 'There is no power on earth that can withstand the united co-operation on spiritual levels of men and women of goodwill everywhere. It is for this reason that the continued and widespread observance of the Silent Minute is of such vital importance in the interest of human welfare.'

Tudor Pole has recently been instrumental in forming the Chalice Well Trust to safeguard and preserve for ever Chalice Well, its gardens and orchards at Glastonbury. Now that it is a reality excavations will be undertaken in the hope of bringing to light many more of the hidden truths, together with historical and archaeological data which have puzzled so many for so long.

It can be seen then that his work for humanity is not only on a very high level, but on a very practical one too. He is, indeed, a veritable 'lighthouse'. Through the light that radiates from him others are drawn into the same work. A good example of what I mean is his vision in founding and carrying on the Silent Minute which has had a wonderful effect on thousands of people.

The amazing experiences he describes and the subjects he discusses in this compelling and extraordinary book, whether dealing with Seership, Prevision, Memory,

Imagination or Dreams, all treat different aspects of the mind. They are parts of the whole and are truly facets of *The Silent Road* along which we all eventually travel towards an ultimate and sometimes unknown goal.

I feel that when the reader does reluctantly come to the end of this volume, his consciousness will have been uplifted by the compassion, wisdom and understanding contained within it as written by a most remarkable man.

London, S.W.1.
January, 1960.

PART I

Chapter One

Passers By

MAN'S LIFE ON earth is of short duration. Viewed from the background of history it is literally true to say that we are here today and gone tomorrow.

We come into this world.
We remain here for a little while.
Then we go away.

Where have we come from? For what purposes are we here? What happens next?

For those who think that man's existence as a conscious being begins at birth and ends at 'death' these questions are meaningless. For the rest of us, they are surely of great importance and cannot be side-stepped or dismissed outright. The teaching contained in the Jewish and Christian Scriptures is preoccupied to a large extent with the need for man to prepare himself now for carrying on his life beyond the grave. Such teaching is not concerned with the past or with belief in the pre-existence of the soul.

On the authority of its Founder, the Christian Faith assures us that eternal life is God's gift to man. The word 'eternal' can only have one meaning, namely, 'without beginning and without end'. If this be the case, surely it is impossible to think that life for you and for me commenced when we were born into this world on the present occasion and that its 'eternality' refers to the future only and not to the past as well?

In spite of the assertions of the materialist to the contrary, it is my conviction that few people really believe in their hearts that life for them is limited to the period between their arrival in this world and their departure from it.

Most of us reject instinctively the idea that we are doomed to extinction when the form we now inhabit decays and dies.

There are certain indications in the New Testament which suggest that Jesus and those around Him accepted the implication that man as a living soul did not start his career when born into this world. This belief, however, is not now or since the 6th Century, a recognised doctrine of the Church. On the other hand, continuation of 'life after death' is a fundamental thesis without which Christian teaching would have little, if any, purpose.

This being the case, it may seem surprising that the Scriptures contain no clear guidance about the conditions and circumstances to be expected when our present life is over! No doubt the explanation is that Revelation is a progressive process and that knowledge concerning the eternal verities reaches human consciousness by stages, being regulated by the rate at which spiritual perception unfolds within each one of us individually. Although the doctrine of Reincarnation or a succession of lives here and elsewhere has never been accepted by those who formulated the Christian creeds, it is basic in the teaching and outlook of the principal oriental faiths. Certain experiences related in the following pages would suggest that it may be worth while to examine this belief with care. There are those who assert that the limitation of man's present knowledge on matters of this kind is fixed by some kind of divine ordinance. For instance, I have been warned by theologians of repute that any attempt to pierce the veil between life on earth and life in other states of consciousness is a sinful practice. One would almost conclude that on a subject of such overwhelming importance to us all we are expected to remain satisfied with the vague generalities concerning Heaven and the after-life that are contained in the Christian Scriptures.

I never cease to be amazed at the lack of serious curiosity shown by so many people in regard to the purpose of their lives either here or in a future state. I cannot remember a time when my desire to know where and how I lived before I was born into this world was not as insistent as my wish to obtain reliable information about the conditions of life I am likely to meet after the death of my physical body.

The injunction to 'Seek and ye shall find' is surely applicable to the region of knowledge that lies beyond the immediate confines of our present state of existence?

There is a saying attributed to Jesus which is recorded in an early Coptic script found at Nag Hamadi, Egypt, some years ago. According to this saying, Jesus enjoined those around him to learn how to regard their present existence on earth from the standpoint of a traveller in transit. (And Jesus said: 'Learn to become Passers By.'*) This would suggest the wisdom of regarding life on earth as a temporary phase in a journey that acts as a link between a pre-existence and a future life. In my view such an attitude of mind can become the first step towards the extension of our perceptions and the widening of our understanding.

It is my hope that the sharing of my personal experience in this field of research may prove of some service to those who are seeking but who have not yet found.

* *The Gospel according to Thomas.*

CHAPTER TWO

An Account of Three Supernatural Experiences

THE FOLLOWING EXPERIENCES have been selected from a large number of similar 'glimpses' into the unseen realms surrounding us—glimpses which have come my way unsought over a long period of years. If they stood alone one might perhaps regard them as coincidental or the fruits of the imagination. I cannot feel that this explanation is adequate, however, in view of their frequency and range of variety; and also the fact that no artificial or automatic methods were employed to bring them about. My views on the use of trance mediumship, automatism and the possession of one individual's mind and person by a disembodied intelligence are referred to elsewhere. I have never felt that such methods were desirable or likely to bring true enlightenment in any permanent sense on the problems of our life on earth or on the conditions awaiting us when we depart elsewhere.

Even if the reader is inclined to disagree with such a sweeping statement, it should be admitted I think that the use of natural and perceptive clairvoyance, the fruit of discipline and training is less dangerous, less illusory and more evolutionary in character than methods which involve the domination of one mind by another.

Each of the three experiences now to be related falls into its own category.

The first deals with the return of a lady who had 'died' some years before the events in question took place. As you will see, she was drawn back to earth levels through the link forged by her great love for her husband and son.

The second is an experience during which a man living in the flesh was able to transport all that made up himself with the exception of his bodily form over a distance of some two thousand miles in order to fulfil a healing mission.

And the third relates to a being who lived on earth some five centuries ago and who appears to be still in contact with our level of consciousness.

Love's Victory Over Death

In 1912 I was spending a holiday on the South Coast of Devon. One Sunday morning I walked through country lanes to attend an early Communion service at a village church some miles away from my hotel. I had not visited this church before and its rector and congregation were complete strangers to me. The rector was elderly and frail in appearance. About a dozen members of the congregation accompanied me to the steps before the altar to partake of the bread and wine. Much to my astonishment, when the rector handed me the cup he stooped down and asked me, in a whisper, to join him in the vestry when the service was over. This I did and found the old man in a state of considerable agitation. He made no attempt to explain his strange behaviour, but at once began to tell me of his distress over the conduct of his only son, nineteen years of age, who since his mother's death some years earlier had taken to drink and other bad habits, thereby causing much scandal in the village and the countryside around. In some bewilderment I enquired in what way I, as a complete stranger, could be of service. I was then asked to accompany this agitated clergyman to his rectory and to take breakfast there with him and his son. To this I agreed, puzzled rather than alarmed, and thinking that perhaps my presence might bring solace to a man who was evidently suffering from a sense of sorrow and unhappiness.

When we entered the hall, I was shown an enlarged coloured photograph of the rector's wife which was hanging on the wall, and for whom he evidently felt a deep and lasting affection. Soon after we sat down to breakfast, the boy came in from a morning ride. He was a tall handsome fellow, but it was not difficult to see that he was already under the influence of drink. He sat silent throughout the meal and then rose abruptly and left the room. His father gave me further particulars of the sad events that had followed his wife's death, and begged me to have a talk with his boy before I went my way.

On entering the boy's study, I found him sitting before his desk, silent and morose, with a decanter of whisky at his elbow. Conversation seemed to be impossible. Quite unexpectedly, his mother, whom I recognised from her photograph, came into the room. She went over and placed her hand upon the boy's shoulder and then turned to me and said quite clearly: 'Please help my darling lad through the terrible trouble that is coming to him.' This gave me the opportunity I was waiting for, and I said, 'Noel, do you know that your mother is in the room?' The reaction was immediate, the boy turned very white, took up the whisky decanter and threw it through the window. He then buried his face in his hands and wept. Realising that he was in no fit state to talk, I took out a card and wrote on it the following message, which I placed on the desk before him: 'I am staying at the . . . Hotel and if you need me let me know and I will come.'

I then went my way after saying goodbye to the boy's father, whom I was not destined to see alive again. At breakfast next morning a violent quarrel broke out between father and son. (The latter told me this later.) The son left the house, jumped on his horse and rode off in a rage. The old man appears to have retired to his study and during the morning fell dead from a stroke. There he remained, undiscovered, until the boy, returning for lunch, stumbled over his father's body lying just within the study door. Evidently he had been trying to reach the bell. In a fit of remorse, the boy then went to his own room and took down from the wall a sporting rifle, with the intention, he told me afterwards, of killing himself. Whilst loading the gun, he happened to see my card which was still lying on his desk. He threw down the rifle and went to the stables, where he remounted his horse and rode over to fetch me. I went back to the rectory with him and stayed there until after the funeral. (Subsequently Noel became my ward, pulled himself together, entered the Army and died courageously whilst bringing in a wounded man from no man's land in France in 1916.)

At the funeral service the mother again came and spoke to me. She said that she had 'come back' to help her husband across the Valley of Darkness, having realised that his earthly end was near. She said she was able to impress her husband sufficiently to enable him to speak to the only member of the congregation on that particular morning whom she believed could intervene in such a way as to avert a double tragedy. Her deep gratitude made me feel very humble, because it was only with reluctance that I had accepted the rector's invitation to breakfast.

Surely we can believe that, under certain circumstances, the bond of love can transcend 'death'?

A Healing Mission

We now come to an experience of a very different kind. In 1919 I was living in a houseboat on the Nile. Apart from my Berberine servants, there was no one else on board. An occasion arose when a virulent fever laid me low and to such an extent that I could not make my servants understand that I wanted one of them to go down the river to Cairo to fetch a doctor.

Whilst lying on my bunk, some seven days after the illness began, I heard a distinct knock on the cabin door. This was followed by the entry of a man who was evidently an Englishman of the professional class. Being in the height of summer, I remember wondering in a hazy way why my visitor was dressed in such unsuitable clothing for the climate, as he was wearing a frock coat and thick striped trousers. He carried a top hat in one hand and a stick and small black bag in the other.

My visitor greeted me pleasantly and sat down on the side of my bunk. I distinctly felt his weight upon the bed. Concluding that he must be a doctor, possibly sent out to see me from the Residency, I thanked him for calling, but added that he had come too late. He took no notice of this remark, but, after studying me closely, advised me to tell one of my servants to go to the Mousque at Cairo and to bring back from a herbalist's shop there a certain remedy for which he gave me the details. This herbal compound was to be infused in hot water and taken three times daily and I was to drink pure lemon juice but to take no solid food of any kind.

I should have mentioned that on entering my cabin this visitor had placed his hat and stick on a small table behind which stood a mirror. During our conversation I happened to look at his hat and, to my surprise, found that I could see the mirror through it. Only then did it dawn on me that my visitor was not bodily present in the accepted meaning of the term. I asked him who he was and where he came from. He replied that he was a British doctor in regular practice. For some time past he said he had been in the habit of locking the door of his consulting room for an hour each evening, stilling his mind and, in prayer, asking that he might be sent wherever he could prove most useful. He added that he rarely remembered his experiences subsequently, although he always knew whether they had proved fruitful or not. After assuring me that I should soon be fit again (which forecast was fulfilled) he wished me well and went away.

Still not being sure that my visitant had not been present in the flesh, I rang for my servant and asked whether he had escorted the doctor safely ashore. In surprise he assured me that no one had come on board throughout the day. I then sent my cook into Cairo, where he succeeded in finding the herbalist's shop and in bringing back the remedy that had been prescribed.

Whether following the instructions related above resulted in my cure or whether this was brought about by the doctor's healing presence is a problem I have never solved, but the intervention described above undoubtedly saved my life.

On returning to London the following year, I tried to trace my visitor by every means in my power, but failed to do so. However, I induced the B.B.C. to allow me to broadcast an account of the experience under the heading 'The strangest thing that has ever happened to me' and this was transmitted in one of their Home Service programmes.

Some weeks later I received a confidential letter from a general practitioner in Scotland, who has long since passed away. He told me that he was in the habit, on specific occasions, of leaving his body and travelling wherever 'he was sent'. He added that he had no recollection of having ever visited Egypt in this way, but that he knew of a colleague of his in Belfast who followed the same practice and that they often compared notes. He begged me to regard his disclosures as confidential because he had no desire to be struck off the Medical Register. Next time I was in Scotland I called at his address but he was away, and when I wrote subsequently his son, who was also a doctor, replied that his father had died whilst on a sea voyage for his health. It turned out that the son knew nothing about his father's supernatural experiences and so, unfortunately, I was obliged to let the matter drop.

The Monk of Tintern Abbey

The incident now to be related is, in my view, the most interesting of the three.

In June 1925 I was staying with a friend at Tintern in South Wales. We were much interested in the Abbey ruins there and spent a good deal of time in examining them and their surroundings. One evening whilst sitting on an ancient stone within the Abbey precincts, I became aware of the presence of a monk, venerable and charming who seemed anxious to enter into conversation. He called himself Brother Brighill. My friend did not see him, but acted as an amanuensis in jotting down the conversation that followed.

Perhaps I should have explained earlier that I am always fully conscious during such experiences as those I am relating. They came and still come to me spontaneously, unexpectedly and quite naturally. There is never any question of abnormality or trance conditions on such occasions.

Only recently my friend's notebook containing details of this particular experience came into my hands, after his own death, and this is why I am reminded of the episode. I cannot do better than set down extracts from this notebook, because the contents were recorded at the time and are therefore more reliable than the use of memory unaided could be, and especially so in view of the lapse of time since these events took place.

Brother Brighill's Story

Here, therefore, are extracts from the diary in question:

June 10th, 1925.

At the end of the fifteenth or beginning of the sixteenth century there lived at Tintern Brother Dominic, a great initiate and scholar of princely family, being of royal French and English blood. He had frequented both courts. Having had the misfortune accidentally to kill a man, he retired from the world and received absolution from the Bishop of Reading. He was a great scholar, linguist and calligraphist, as well as an illuminator of missals. He first entered Tintern as a lay brother, but later became a brother and then Librarian and Custodian of Records. People from all parts came to him to decipher old documents: even I fetched over from Glastonbury to Tintern records for his inspection and advice. The name Brother Dominic hid a very well-known and historic personage.

The stream (which runs down the hill) was once called the Brig, but later became known as the Stream of the Fish because a salmon had managed extraordinarily to climb or jump up the stream to the top of the hill and was caught by monks in the pond there. Upon the fish being opened, a tiny circle of gold was found inside it. No doubt owing to the Abbey's connection with the Fish symbol, a special mystic significance was attributed to the event, and because of it the hill and stream then became known as the Hill and Stream of the Fish. There was once healing power in the stream, and radio-activity, but apparently it has not now the same qualities, and the volume and level of the water is lower.

In a later conversation, Brother Brighill gave us the following information:

June 11th, 1925.

There is still extant in the mountains of central South America a race of very small men with clairvoyant and other powers not usual to men on earth. This race had its roots in Egypt and south of Egypt and migrated across Atlantis. These men are now fair, almost flaxen, though tanned. They are very good men, directly God-inspired. They are not what you call civilised. The black men who surround them regard them as gods and keep travellers at bay, thinking they would lose their good fortune and protection if their 'gods' were not protected. The mountains are snow-capped but the valleys are warm. Among the black men they are supposed to guard great treasure. If you ever visit South America you will hear of the quest for the great white race. When a new race comes about in the New World, they will be its inspirers. I once visited them. They built up a body for me. They are one of the centres of illumination which have helped to keep the light in the world. They do not generate physically They are quite a small number, and come and go without the need of incarnation.

June 12th, 1925.

There is excitement just now I understand about great scientific discoveries in Germany and the United States of America, and there is someone in England who is nearly at the same point (scientifically) as the group in Germany. The discovery is a chemical one in Germany and of an 'electrical' nature in the United States of America. The scientists are being held back as the time is not ripe. One of the teachers of the race of white men had to work on these discoveries and 'send the seed out'. I see no cataclysm ahead. An earthquake was diverted the other day but no cataclysms. You have misinterpreted the symbols. The white men referred to above use the Fish symbol and also that of the Chalice.

THREE SUPERNATURAL EXPERIENCES

The following Incantation against evil forces was given by Brother Brighill on another occasion:

In the name of the White Cross and of the Pentagram of the Red Rose, I command thee to depart from hence and be transmuted from darkness into Light. In the name of God, His Christ and of all Holy Souls. *Amen.*

Next day Brother Brighill came to us and spoke as follows:

June 13, 1925.

There were four chapels in my time [at Tintern], 116 years from the building of the present edifice. The Blessed Mother, St. Peter, St. George right of the High Altar in the transept, St. Thomas and St. Luke the Healer in the West Aisle of the nave. In the Abbot's private chapel there was an altar dedicated to the Four Archangels. At a later time the chapels were dedicated afresh and to other saints —much, much after my time, near the Reformation. These were not the only saints honoured in the Abbey, and the Holy Mother was much revered here. There were wonderful bells and there was a belfry. It was not the central tower of the Abbey buildings. There was an altar in the novices' lodgings dedicated to Holy Souls. It was a place of inspiration for the novices. A small pulpit was there. The term 'lodgment' is not exact. In my time there was a great oak tree growing near the lodgings and a small garden. It was such a long time ago I may not be quite exact as to details but I shall do the best I can. There was no village but only a few homesteads—several small farms near the hills and houses and a castle near where the Wye joined the Severn [Chepstow].

Brother Brighill then related how a young man who was condemned to death at Chepstow (for stealing a loaf of bread), was first put into the stocks. The Abbot saw him there and begged the governor of the castle to pardon him, which he did, and then sent him to the Abbey where he became a lay brother. Later, by special dispensation, owing to his eloquence, he became a wandering friar and used to come to the Abbey once in a while. He died in old age and was buried here. Eloquent in spiritual things, he was clear-seeing and at times prophetical. He became known as Friar John. He went once so far afield as Reading and London and was oft at Gloucester in the market place and even in the churches. Brother Brighill thinks he can show where he was buried. Behold what a good deed of charity can do! He never learnt to read or write. He made a prophecy at a service in the novices' room to the brothers, 'that a time would come when the river would diminish, a town would spring up, the Abbey Church would lie in ruins, new rulers would be in the land, the common people would be their own masters, there would be no more ordinary servants but many slaves to machines. This and other of God's houses would be in ruins and Orders dispersed. Great battles would be fought out in foreign lands, ships would move with wheels, they would fly like birds, coaches would run on rails. The climate would change. Voices raised in the praise of God would be little heard. Our Holy Hill would be forgotten.

'There would be myriads of men in the Isles where there are now thousands so that they could not feed and support themselves from their own gardens or from the common store. Then a sign would come in many holy centres, and in this one too [Tintern] and at Avalon new life would spring. The birth of Jesus, the Christ, and of His life and His word would become freshly known once more, turning men's minds from earth to heavenly things. Light would appear at those centres where the symbol of the Holy Fish was honoured. This day is afar off and all its wonders cannot be told now, but out of the darkness will come a great light and from the womb of God will come forth once more the shining of His Spirit.'

THREE SUPERNATURAL EXPERIENCES

In the course of further conversation Brother Brighill stated that this sermon caused a great commotion, many of the brothers thought that Friar John was mad and their minds went back to his early history.

The Abbot caused him to be protected, although it was long before he allowed him to journey forth again to preach the word of God in the countryside. No name was placed on his tomb when he came to be buried. The Holy Fish was inscribed thereon and the letter J. Upon being asked questions, Brother Brighill stated that the prophecy was in the Abbot's diary or journal, which he thinks was destroyed. One reference to it, however, was to be found. It was not here (Tintern). It was on the fly-leaf of a Latin missal belonging to a Monk Alban, now in a room (museum?) in a private house of a Catholic household. It is here (i.e., the missal) that a reference is made to these prophecies. This Monk Alban was on a visit from Llanthony and was told the story whilst he was at Tintern Abbey.

Brother Brighill concluded his conversation with us by saying:

> Where a prophecy concerning great spiritual matters is made it is usual by the hand of Providence for a record to be kept for the use of future ages and it may be so in this instance.

Brother Brighill stated that he was alive at the time of the blessed Joan and was middle-aged at the time of her death. Throughout these conversations with this lively visitant, my companion and I had been sitting on the stone in the Abbey grounds which has been mentioned earlier.

When we came to examine its surface carefully by scraping away the lichen, the faint outline of a fish became visible, also part of a letter which may well have been the letter J.

• • • • • •

I only propose to make short comment here on the value or otherwise of the three experiences given in this chapter. In the first two I think one might be justified in feeling that there was sufficient evidence inherent within the episodes themselves to justify a measure of belief in their validity. This, however, is not true of the third, so far as I am aware. If any historical evidence exists to the effect that a Brother Brighill once lived at Tintern Abbey, so far it has not come to light. On the other hand, several monks and friars belonging to Tintern Abbey in the fourteenth and fifteenth centuries were named John. It may well be that the name Brighill was used colloquially and was not this brother's Christian title. In spite of this fact, the impression left upon me by what seemed to be a genuine conversation with the intelligence calling himself Brother Brighill remains profound. I find it impossible to dismiss the whole experience as fantasy. If it be the latter, then my powers of improvisation must be far more remarkable than I think is at all likely.

Where not given in the context, the names of those connected with the experiences related in this book are available in confidence to serious enquirers.
—W. T. P.

CHAPTER THREE

Further Unusual Incidents

A Puzzling Time Sequence

I NOW COME to a difficult task. This is to describe in intelligible words experiences which to the reader may seem both incredible and inexplicable. I can but relate these happenings exactly as they occurred, and leave it at that.

Some eight years after the end of the second world war, a soldier friend of mine ran into grave trouble. Caught up in a complexity of unusual circumstances, he found himself involved in a case of manslaughter. Technically, and perhaps legally also, the charge against him appeared on the surface to be watertight. Whilst out on bail this unfortunate young man came to consult me confidentially as I was a friend of long standing. He showed me the notes that his legal advisers had prepared for him. In substance their contents indicated that he would be wise to follow the unusual course of pleading guilty, but with extenuating circumstances, and to throw himself on the mercy of the court. Realising instinctively that he was innocent, I felt unable to advise him to plead guilty even if the court allowed him to do so. He seemed inclined to agree with me, but was too perturbed mentally to decide for himself then one way or the other. Later, however, he did decide to plead 'Not guilty'.

The trial was due to open on a certain Thursday at a court in Britain that shall be nameless, because those intimately concerned are still alive. On the preceding Tuesday, affairs called me abroad and I left England filled with foreboding for my friend. I arrived in Genoa about noon on the Wednesday and went straight to my hotel. After lunch I retired to my room to write letters, but found that I was too upset to be able to concentrate on correspondence. I went out on to the balcony overlooking the harbour—one of the most interesting sights in Europe—and sat down there to enjoy the view. The time was about 2 p.m. local time, equivalent to noon in London. Unexpectedly I found myself in an English court of law listening to the pleadings in a case of manslaughter. I should explain that I was not asleep in the normal sense, because the noises from the harbour and the cries of the seabirds continued to ring in my ears. As the case proceeded I realised with a start that it concerned my friend, who at the moment was writing a note to his solicitor. Realising that it was Wednesday and that the case was not due to begin until the next day, I came to the conclusion that for some unexpected reason the case had been put forward by twenty-four hours. It soon became evident that in the light of the evidence being given a conviction was almost inevitable, and I roused myself without listening further and returned to full consciousness of my surroundings in Genoa. Curiously enough, even then I continued to hear snatches of talk from the court, comments by the judge and interchange of passages between opposing counsel. As there was no telephone in my room I went down into the hotel lobby and put through a call to my London office. The time was now about 4.30 p.m., or 2.30 p.m. in London. On getting through to London I asked my secretary to find out why the case in question had been put forward by a day. Half an hour later he rang me back to say that the case had not yet begun but would open as originally arranged at 11 a.m. the next day (Thursday). This news staggered me and brought me to the conclusion that my experience had simply resulted from the vagaries of imagination. Some hours later, whilst at dinner, it came to me quite clearly that, as a result of what I had heard of the first day's hearing, my friend was doomed to a verdict of 'Guilty' unless he changed the whole course of his defence. I got up from dinner and telephoned to a colleague who I knew could gain access to the accused the same night. I asked him to advise an entire change of defence policy: this to consist in refusing the services of defending counsel, ignoring all the carefully prepared legal arguments on his behalf and going into the witness-box on his own account, unhampered by any previous 'coaching'. There he should relate in simple language his version of the events leading up to the tragedy and his own part in them, being careful not to defend his conduct in any way or to appear to be seeking a verdict of 'Not guilty'. After listening to all this, my colleague, who was not a lawyer (neither am I) but possessed a good measure of legal experience, began to expostulate with me. He said that it would be madness to follow the advice I offered. In any case, he pointed out that until the trial had begun the next morning, no one could predict the arguments and the evidence that would be put forward by prosecuting counsel. I realised that it was useless for me to assure him that I had already heard these arguments and had summed up in my mind the dangerous effect they would have upon both judge and jury. Finally I persuaded my colleague to pass on to the threatened man the advice I had tendered. He saw him late that night and telephoned me early next morning to say that the course I had suggested was likely to be followed, adding that he himself had warned the accused of the dangers involved by such unwise and unprecedented action. I went down to an early breakfast on that Thursday morning, only wishing that over seven hundred miles did not separate me from the scene of action. My colleague's final words the evening before kept ringing in my ears. 'What on earth is the good of spending over £1,000 on legal advice and then throwing it all over at the eleventh hour?' I left for Rome that morning and during the long and dusty journey I did all possible to project myself into that court again. In this I failed. Perhaps if the place had been familiar I might have succeeded, but I had never visited it in the flesh. Usually people rather than places afford the best 'links', but not always. On reaching Rome very late that night I managed to contact my London secretary, who was annoyed at being roused from sleep. He had heard that the case was going very badly for my friend, but he had no idea as to what line the defence was likely to take. On the Friday I was too absorbed by business affairs to secure any quiet, but towards evening a sense of peace came over me and I knew that all was well. I heard afterwards that my advice had been followed, much to the anger of the legal pundits. To everyone's complete surprise, a verdict of 'Not guilty' was brought in at four-fifteen London time on that Friday afternoon. Due to telephone delays, the good news did not reach me in Naples, where I then was, until midday on the Saturday. However, it had already reached me interiorly and its confirmation came as no surprise. When back in London a week later, I was able to read through the transcript of the court proceedings. The gist of what I had heard and seen on the Wednesday afternoon had actually taken place some twenty hours later and over seven hundred miles away. In some strange way I had forestalled 'time' through the faculty of prevision.

As most of those intimately concerned with the events

just described are still alive, I have felt it only fair to disguise to some extent both venue and personalities. For the same reason I can offer readers no corroborative evidence to support my story. Take it or leave it, but if taken seriously a very interesting line of research is opened up.

Transit Most Mysterious

And now for another experience which also involves the time factor.

On a wet and stormy night in December 1952, I found myself at a country station some mile and a half from my Sussex home. The train from London had arrived late, the bus had gone and no taxis were available. The rain was heavy and incessant. The time was 5.55 p.m. and I was expecting an important trunk call from overseas at 6 p.m. at home. The situation seemed desperate. To make matters worse, the station call box was out of order and some trouble on the line made access to the railway telephone impossible. In despair I sat down in the waiting-room and, having nothing better to do, I compared my watch with the station clock. Allowing for the fact that this is always kept two minutes in advance, I was able to confirm the fact that the exact time was then 5.57 p.m. Three minutes to zero hour! What happened next I cannot say. When I came to myself I was standing in my hall at home, a good twenty minutes' walk away, and the clock was striking six. My telephone call duly came through a few minutes later. I should have explained that I had set out that morning minus both coat and umbrella. It had been a fine morning but by early evening the downpour had become almost tropical. Having finished my call, I awoke to the realisation that something very strange had happened. Then, much to my surprise, I found that my shoes were dry and free from mud, and that my clothes showed no sign of damp or damage. My housekeeper looked at me somewhat strangely at supper that night, but no word was said. Indeed, what 'word' was there to say?

A Ring of Surprise

When Allenby's forces entered Haifa in 1918 I made it my first duty to visit the Persian prophet Abdul Baha Abbas, leader of the Bahai movement, who at that time was residing on the slopes of Mount Carmel. I was relieved to find that the measures we had taken to ensure his and his followers' safety had proved successful. This benevolent and saintly man, to whom I shall be referring again later in this book, presented me with a signet ring on which was inscribed in Persian the names and titles of God. Before giving me the ring, Abdul Baha blessed it in a very special way. It thus became a precious possession and never left my finger.

Soon after the Armistice in November 1918, whilst I was living on a dahabieh on the Nile, not far from the Gizeh pyramids, a message reached me from the Residency at Cairo. I was asked to call there on the following afternoon to meet a very distinguished Englishman and his wife. This I did and took the opportunity of inviting the famous pair to take tea with me on my boat. To this they agreed and we enjoyed a very pleasant afternoon. Later, as it was a fine evening, I suggested that the Residency car, which had brought us from Cairo to Gizeh, should be dismissed. I then offered to sail my visitors down the Nile to the Residency steps about a mile away and on the opposite side of the river. For this purpose two of my Berberine servants manned the felucca and so soon as my guests were safely on board I took the tiller and we set forth briskly, helped along by the usual evening wind from the south. The Nile was in flood, the current strong, and my whole attention was centred on steering and on watching the way in which my servants managed the considerable span of sail. We are now coming to the central focus of a very strange experience. When we were in mid-stream and about a quarter of a mile from our destination, a shot rang out. At that moment my attention was distracted by an unusually violent gust of wind which resulted in the felucca losing its equilibrium. I took one hand off the tiller to reach for a trailing rope and in so doing the precious and unique ring described above slipped from my finger and disappeared into the water at a point where the Nile was deepest. Gone for ever. . . . Only then did I see that the bullet must have passed within two feet of my head and that its passage had rent a small hole in the sail. The gun had evidently been fired from marshland on Roda Island, but no one was to be seen there. I should have explained that at the time British officers were unpopular in Egypt and on several previous occasions I had been fired at in the narrow streets of Cairo. Had I not been in uniform the incident described might never have occurred. Fortunately my passengers, Lord and Lady X, had noticed nothing and our journey was completed safely. Then I sailed back to my dahabieh, a sad and disappointed man. The sense of loss seemed more than I could bear.

When I awoke the next morning I found myself saying, over and over again. 'Pray for all you are worth and all will be well'. This injunction remained with me during the next three months and I did my best to believe that nothing is impossible in answer to deep prayer and profound faith. At that time my office was situated in the British Military H.Q. at the Savoy Hotel in Cairo and was on the top floor at the back of the building, being faced on the opposite side of the street by a tall block of flats with balconies. The city was still in a very disturbed state and British officers had been warned to dress in mufti as often as official regulations permitted. One late afternoon, at about the same time as my ring had fallen into the Nile three months before, I was sitting at my desk in shirt-sleeves, the double windows of my room being wide open. Suddenly a shot rang out, apparently fired from a balcony across the street. The bullet missed me by two feet or so and embedded itself in the wall facing the windows. At that very moment my ring fell down upon the blotter on the desk in front of me with a sharp thud. It was intact in every way and is still in my possession.

For those who believe in the theory of the materialisation and the dematerialisation of objects and their transportation across space whilst remaining in invisible 'form', there is one point about this very unlikely tale that will interest them.

The time and conditions associated with the loss of the ring were duplicated as nearly as may be when the ring reappeared. The hour of day, the weather, and the transit of a bullet were all repeated, the main difference being of course that the loss took place in the water and in the open air, and the recovery took place on land and in a room. Yes, there are certainly 'more things in Earth and Heaven' than can be conceived by man in his present state of spiritual and mental infancy.

An Aftermath of Suicide

The following incident is one of several others of a similar kind that have come my way and may be worth recording here.

When living in Hampstead some years ago, the wife of a business friend called upon me in great distress. Her husband had been missing for two days and she feared that he was suffering from loss of memory. Realising instinctively that the situation was more serious than appeared to be the case, I offered my help in trying to trace the missing man.

His wife told me that her husband was in good health and had no business worries so far as she knew. Having done my best to calm her agitation I accompanied her home after promising to get into touch with the police on her behalf.

On the evening of the same day I returned with the intention of enquiring whether any news had been received meanwhile. When approaching the house I noticed that someone was trying ineffectually to unlatch the garden gate, and on closer inspection it turned out to be the missing man himself. He was drenched to the skin and was shivering violently. Turning to me he said, 'I am so cold and frightened and am longing to be dry again and to get into a warm bed, but I cannot seem to open this gate'. It was not until I had done this for him and watched his progress towards the front door of his home that I realised what had happened. My friend had been drowned but evidently was quite unaware of the fact. At the moment there seemed no way in which I could intervene, mainly because no objective confirmation of my impression was forthcoming. I went home and spent some time in prayer both for him and his distracted wife. Then I rang her up with the intention of trying to soften the blow if by chance an intimation of the truth had reached her. She said there was no news, but she felt that something terrible had happened. Would I get into touch with the police again? This I did, and without giving my reason intimated that the missing man might have been drowned and suggested that search be made in the Thames and elsewhere near London, with this idea in mind. Meanwhile there seemed no useful purpose in sharing my apprehensions with the wife or with anyone else. After all it was just possible that I might be mistaken in my interpretation of the position.

Next day my friend's body was recovered from the Thames and a verdict of suicide was duly recorded, with the rider that no evidence was available as to the state of his mind at the time. His affairs were in good order and he had always enjoyed a happy home life; in fact no explanation of his action was forthcoming either then or subsequently. After the cremation I accompanied the widow to her house, doing all that was possible to relieve her grief.

Two days later when passing his house on my way home from the City, I met my friend once more. As on the previous occasion, he was standing in the road outside his own gate trying to get in. He still had no idea that he was 'dead' and complained that he felt as if he were on fire and feared that he was suffering from fever. It seemed wise to try to make him understand what had happened to him and to keep him company until some measure of comprehension dawned. This proved a difficult task, but was accomplished in the end through the loving aid of his own brother who had died some years earlier and who was able to come to his rescue at this time of tragic crisis.

I have related this experience exactly as it happened. There has seemed no good cause, either then or since, to pass on the details to his widow or to anyone else concerned. In a matter of this kind it would be impossible to divulge names without causing needless suffering, and it is for this reason that I have disguised some of the details in order to preserve anonymity.

In cases of sudden and premature death, especially when resulting from suicide, it would seem wise to delay cremation, if that form of disposal of the body be desired, for at least seven days after 'death'. This should give ample time for complete disassociation to take place.

As our knowledge of other worldly conditions grows and becomes more generally understood I feel convinced that the suicide rate will begin to decline. The man who destroys his own body must expect to remain earthbound at least until his natural span on earth would have been completed. In the meantime the conditions of his existence in the shadow realm 'between heaven and earth' will prove to be extremely difficult and unrewarding.

It is to be hoped that the relating of such incidents as the above may prove helpful to those who feel tempted to end their earth lives prematurely.

No evidence has reached me to suggest that harmful effects follow cremation where death has been due to natural causes; in fact I have arranged for my own body to be cremated when I have no further use for its services.

The grave injury to the community resulting from capital punishment is rarely recognised. When the body of a murderer is hanged or electrocuted his unregenerate mind lives on, clothed in a body that is invisible to earthly sight. Inevitably he remains earthbound, perhaps for a long period, with his desires unsatisfied and unabated. It is not unusual for a man who has committed an unpremeditated murder to confess that he felt himself compelled to do it and that he acted automatically.

Are we so sure that on many such occasions the impulse to kill did not result from a powerful but unseen incitement, an incitement inspired by a former murderer already 'dead'? The destruction of the body of one who is obsessed by evil impulses solves nothing and may indeed result in an increase of such crimes.

For this reason it may well be that the use of capital punishment by the State is in itself a crime against the community as a whole.

Chapter Four

Memory, Time and Prevision

Being the substance of an Address given in London in 1943.

THERE ARE THREE subjects closely related to one another which can be summed up in three words: MEMORY, TIME and PREVISION.

MEMORY can be defined as the faculty of the mind by which it can retain and recall previous ideas and impressions. It is therefore associated with the past, whereas prevision belongs to the future. The passage of time links the past and the future within the immediate *now* which in reality contains them both. This fact should, I think, give us the clue to the relation between memory and prevision, and may indeed indicate that they represent two sides of the same coin.

It is strange that neither Religion nor Science has so far been able to throw light upon one of the most amazing faculties of the human mind; that is, the power or gift of memory. In fact memory is far more than a power or a gift, and we do not know what it is nor do we know anything about the agency or medium which acts as an intermediary between mind and brain through which memory operates. Our knowledge is so small in this field of research that we have not yet discovered the method by which a thought impresses itself upon the physical brain, how the brain reacts to this impression, nor by what process a thought-wave is translated through the brain into an external act. According to one theory the brain, or its subtle counterpart, contains within itself some apparatus that can be compared to the sensitised film or plate used in photography on which every thought, feeling or event experienced by the individual is indelibly recorded. Think what this means! Every hour of the day, hundreds, perhaps thousands of impressions are recorded in this way and are stored up in some mysterious manner capable of being brought to light again when the human will calls memory into play. For instance perhaps twenty years hence you and I will be able to recollect, if we so will, the thoughts and experiences that come to us as we are gathered here this evening.

According to Eastern lore there also exists what might be termed 'planetary memory', which includes within itself a record of the acts and experiences of all forms of life that have ever existed upon this earth. These records are said to be our common heritage and the foundation upon which individual memory is built. For instance, the combination of ideas which form the basis of 'new' discoveries are thought to proceed from this universal reservoir that is available to be drawn upon whenever the need arises.

In any case it seems that nothing is ever lost. Every idea or impression received through all or any of the five senses during every minute of the day is recorded automatically and can be brought back into view through the exercise of what is called memory. It is true that we are forgetful creatures and therefore disinclined to believe that all we think and do is indelibly stored in the mind in this way. And yet it often happens that some chance remark will bring a flood of memory into play concerning long-forgotten incidents, sometimes of quite trivial character, showing clearly that everything that happens is registered permanently.

This amazing fact brings us to the consideration of time itself and the relation between time and memory.

Time used to be regarded as a kind of ever-unrolling scroll or thread upon which all human and planetary events were inscribed as and when they happened. According to this concept time in the past tense was fixed, all happenings within its orbit being unalterable. It was considered that time in the present tense was fluid and not necessarily affected by either past or future events. This conception has been modified considerably and 'Time' is now regarded *as if it were a whole*, in which is included past, present and future as a completed unit. Instead of time in the future sense being virgin, like a series of blank sheets in a book, it is now believed by many that what we call the future 'in time' is not only already in existence but is already filled with the impression of events that in a human sense have not yet taken place. It is as if time were in the form of a closed circle rather than a spiral that is so far as life on this planet is concerned and consequently happenings at any point in the circle, past, present or future, are so closely interrelated that in a certain manner, past, present and future are included and operative in the NOW. In this connection it seems well to remember that there are many different forms of what we call 'time'.

To the Creator, viewing His creation from the standpoint of eternity, a thousand years may seem but as a day. Then we have the Divine promise assuring us that our calls will be heard and answered *before* they are made, which indicates a conception of time that is unfamiliar to most of us.

You will have noticed that the relation of time to events as experienced in dreams is of quite a different order to solar 'time' and in the use of memory we can vary the duration of past happenings at will so that in such instances time becomes our servant instead of our master. In regard to interior mental and emotional experiences it would seem that each individual possesses a time sense that is his own unique property. It is, I think, well to bear these ideas in mind when discussing time as a link between memory and prevision.

Many of you may have had the experience when taking part in certain events on a given day of having lived through these very events previously, either in dream or waking state. I will give you one of many happenings of this kind in order to illustrate what I mean.

Travelling by train on a route previously unknown I have suddenly become aware that the scenery was familiar and that the stranger sitting opposite was about to make a remark which was already known to me. A conversation ensued every word of which was familiar recalled by the memory of these very incidents, as if they had already happened once before, perhaps many years previously. As the train proceeded the view from the windows conformed with what had previously been foreseen and was related to the conversation between the stranger and myself, also foreseen or foreknown in every particular.

One explanation put forward in recent times suggests that the subconscious registers external impressions a fraction of a second before the conscious mind, hence the sense of familiarity shown by the latter in instances of the sort just described. This explanation, however, does not cover the many cases where the prevision of a chain of events precedes their happening externally by a period of anything from twenty-four hours to perhaps twenty-five years or more.

In instances of this kind, which are fairly common, we seem to be faced with the fact that memory is a faculty which can probe into the future as well as into the past. If this be a fact capable of scientific proof, then we are faced by a great mystery. If incidents in human life that have not yet happened 'in time' can be accurately foreseen or lived through in thought or memory *before* they happen, then to what extent are we endowed with free-will? Is every event and experience between the cradle and the grave foredetermined in detail, as would apparently be the case if such events and experiences can be clearly foreseen in advance? Is it possible, given the right conditions, to become aware of happenings that have not yet taken place outwardly, as accurately as we can remember incidents from the past?

The problems of free-will and destiny seem to be insoluble in our present stage of knowledge; in fact the implications of memory, time and prevision are so baffling as to deserve wider study and research than have yet been given to them.

I remember an experience that came to me in Rome some years ago which touches directly on the subject we are discussing.

Walking along one of the main streets of the city, I happened to pass a wine-shop and noticed that a horse and cart were drawn up alongside. It was one of those country carts used for transporting barrels of wine and the driver was standing beside a table saying goodbye to a girl who was evidently his sweetheart. Suddenly, and without previous warning, I felt a strong urge to join them, and to do what I could to delay the young driver's departure. I walked towards them with this intention in view when I heard the voice of someone I could not see saying in solemn tones: 'It is not for you to interfere with Destiny'. Much taken aback I decided not to intervene and went my way. A little later in the Piazza di Populo, I came across a crowd and was told there had been an accident. It appeared that a horse and cart had collided with a tramcar and the horse and driver had been killed. On further investigation it turned out that the driver was the young fellow whose departure from the wine-shop I had felt impelled to delay. The accident took place at a blind corner of the Piazza and even a few moments' delay at the wine-shop would have prevented the cart arriving at that corner at the same moment as the tramcar, in which case, humanly speaking, there would have been no accident.

I do not wish to draw any moral from this experience nor can I explain why the impulse to intervene was overcome by a stronger urge to let well alone. However I am satisfied that I was guided to do the right thing.

Quite a number of similar experiences have come my way and they incline one to the belief that predestination may be a stronger force in human affairs than the power of free-will, anyway in the present stage of human evolution on earth.

It may well be that the faculty of memory, whether consciously exercised or not, together with the records to which memory has access have a greater influence on our actions and our freedom of choice than any other single factor. What we think and do now must be largely the result of what we have thought and done in the past. Free-will, therefore, to the extent that it exists, must surely be subject to a chain of causes and effects, and what is termed 'memory' would appear to be the controlling factor. Perhaps the spirit of man is able to exercise a large measure of freedom of will in the realm of the soul and mind, whereas such freedom is inevitably modified or even banished altogether, through the influence of memory, when it becomes a question of translating thoughts into deeds. If this line of reasoning is tenable, then the study of the power of memory becomes more important than has been realised hitherto.

If memory can be regarded as a decisive link between fate and free-will, then there is another consideration that should not be forgotten. As man grows in spiritual understanding, a time is reached when he is faced with the choice between the continued effort to exercise his own will or submission of his freedom and his fate to the Will of his Creator. It is at this juncture that the greater Mind begins to make its presence felt and he who chooses to obey the Divine Will rather than his own discovers a freedom and a happiness that he has never known before. It is then that personal fate and free-will gradually become merged into something that transcends them both, and the problem we are now discussing ceases to exist.

In connection with the prevision of future events some modern writers have made use of the following illustration.

If a man is walking along a road with high hedges on either side his vision is restricted to that section of the road immediately in view. Let it be supposed that it were possible for him to lift his consciousness into an aeroplane that is travelling overhead. Under such circumstances he would be able to watch himself walking along the road and to see what was going on on either side of it and his vision would also include a far longer stretch of the road than would be possible from ground level. For instance if a motor-car were approaching from round a bend of the road ahead he would be in a position to compute the moment when the car would pass the pedestrian, that is himself, and so to predict certain events before they actually happened in a physical sense. In other words, the power of accurate prediction may largely depend upon the angle and elevation of vision from which the person concerned is looking out on life. However, even if one allows for the possibility that extended vision of this kind is possible under certain circumstances it does not follow that the *interpretation* of the events so perceived will of necessity prove correct.

Perhaps the most remarkable case of prevision which has fallen to my lot happened in 1910, in the Egyptian desert. I had lost my way in the sand, many miles from camp, and was feeling desperate. After some hours of wandering I met an Arab on camel-back who directed me upon my way. Before parting we sat down for a chat and quite unexpectedly my companion began to smooth the sand in front of him with a circular movement of his hands. He then appeared to pass into a trance and in a voice that was not his own began to prophesy. This quite unlettered man whom I had never met before gave an accurate picture of events in my life up to that time and carried on his story over a period which covered both the great wars. His predictions in regard to the part which I and others would play in these upheavals was given in some detail and has proved correct, I might add uncannily so, even in regard to the measurement of the time that would elapse between each event touched upon.

I am well aware that many prophetic utterances of this character turn out to be without foundation in fact, but when accuracy of the kind referred to *is* attained it is only possible to suppose that a little-known clairvoyant faculty does exist in human consciousness through which events and experiences still in the 'future' can be correctly foreseen. The law governing such prevision is unknown and perhaps it is just as well that this is so.

It is of course possible to conceive that 'memory', properly trained, can roam about in time whether it be past, present or future, according to human standards, and can even perceive those happenings that have not yet 'happened'.

Be this as it may, a fairly wide experience extending over fifty years has convinced me that only in very rare cases is there anything of real value to be gained by a knowledge of future events disclosed by the clairvoyant or some other faculty of the human mind. On the contrary, there are dangers associated with the attempt to peer into the future that in my view far outweigh any advantages to be obtained.

In connection with predictions concerning possible future events in the lives of individuals, it often happens that brooding upon such forecasts causes positive harm to the person concerned and engenders a spirit of discontent and restlessness. A lady, famous in the diplomatic world, once told me that when she was a girl a gipsy reading her palm predicted that she would live to nearly four score years and ten and would then meet her end 'in a pillar of fire'. This prophecy created a deep impression and it is possible that the expectation resulting helped to bring about the final tragedy. In her eighty-sixth year, the lady in question, whilst reading a newspaper, fell asleep in front of an open fire, the newspaper was set alight, and the sheet of flame which enveloped her fulfilled the prophecy that had been made seventy years before.

Instances of this kind seem to show the uselessness of seeking information concerning future events and the harm that may result from such experiments.

Turning to another aspect of the same subject, the interest now being shown in Biblical prophecy is widespread. Verses from the Bible and other sacred writings, often torn from their context are being used in an attempt to interpret the course of the present world crisis and its possible aftermath. One must confess that such interpretations are often ingenious and alluring, as is the case when the symbolism of the Great Pyramid is pressed into the service of prophecy. It seems to many, however, that predictions based on 'evidence' of this kind are too conflicting to prove of any real service. Nevertheless so much prominence is given to prophetic utterances in Holy Writ that one must suppose that some spiritual purpose lies behind them. For instance, when the effect of prophecy is to lift our thought towards a higher outlook perhaps in relation to the approach of some spiritual happening of great importance then one can understand how such a prophecy might prove of value and significance. On the other hand it is difficult to see any useful service in predictions relating to disasters and upheavals over which the average person can have no measure of control, because such predictions must tend to lower moral and mental resilience.

It is I think, an interesting and well-attested fact that premonition of death sharpens vision and sometimes releases the gift of prophecy. It may be that when awareness grows that one's days on earth are nearing their end the vision of eternal realities throws a clear light upon past events and even upon happenings that have not yet taken place. The story has often been told of the soldier, fighting in the hills around Jerusalem in 1917, who received a premonition that he would not survive the battle that was to be fought on the following day. In the light of this awareness he was able to look forward twenty-two years in time and to predict the coming of Armageddon which has now descended upon us. That prophetic vision has resulted in the establishment of the 'Silent Minute' which is now so widely observed when Big Ben chimes the hour of nine each evening.

If the approach of physical death does seem in many instances to quicken or extend the range of vision one might expect that the passing-over experience would lead to a still greater measure of insight. What evidence is available in this respect is conflicting. I think it can safely be said that in the vast majority of cases those who have passed into another world are not suddenly endowed with any wider vision than was theirs before. Prophetic messages received from such sources, whether in regard to world events or personal affairs, are rarely more enlightening than similar impressions formed by those who are still dwelling upon the earth. Let me hasten to add that I am only speaking here from my own experience of such communications and that there are many well-attested instances that seem to point the other way. Broadly speaking, however, there is no reason to suppose that the experience of physical death is in itself the gateway to deeper vision, that a man's faculties are necessarily changed or enlarged purely as a result of his exit from bodily conditions. Growth is a slow and evolutionary process wherever one may be.

It is, I think, true to say that the conditions of war and sudden death do seem to thin the veils between our world and that condition of life sometimes called Borderland by which we are invisibly surrounded. Let me give you two instances out of many which could be quoted, to illustrate what I mean.

During the last war a company commander well known to me was killed by a sniper's bullet at the beginning of an engagement in the Palestine hill country. He was so loved by his men that it was decided not to disclose his death until the battle was over. This officer was killed at seven in the morning and yet throughout that day he was seen leading his men into the attack and on several occasions his speech and guidance saved those under his command from ambush and probable annihilation. At the end of the day when the objective had been successfully reached, this officer went among his men and thanked them for their bravery and endurance. He spoke, and was spoken to in a perfectly natural way. It was only later the same night when the men were told that their commanding officer had been killed early that morning that he ceased to be visible to them and even then there were many who could not be convinced that their leader had 'gone west'. This is an experience which I can vouch for personally as I was there, and I know of others of a similar kind.

During the present war, for instance, the following

account was given me by an airman whose level-headedness I have no reason to doubt.

He was briefed to pilot a bomber plane for a raid over a German city. I will quote his own words so far as I can remember them: 'This was my first operational flight, and I was nervous. My squadron leader, for whom I had a great affection, called me aside before we set out and gave me his final instructions. Having done so, he added: "If you get into trouble, signal me and I will look after you." The outward journey was successful, and I dropped my bombs and turned for home. At that moment a flak splinter entered the cockpit and smashed my instruments. I lost touch with the squadron and found myself alone in a fog circling over the North Sea. I had lost my bearings. Oil and petrol were running low. I got through to X and he replied giving me my right course and suggesting methods for making the best use of my petrol reserves. As a result I landed safely at the base. To my amazement I then heard that X had been shot down and killed during the raid, some time *before* I had heard his voice over the R.T. giving me clear directions which undoubtedly saved the lives of myself and my crew. My observer heard and recognised his voice as clearly as I did.'

If there is any moral to be drawn from these experiences I think it is this: the bond of love is stronger than the power of death and under certain circumstances can overcome the barrier which is caused by death. Were these isolated incidents they might be explained away, but many more of a similar kind could be quoted to suggest that physical death in itself does not necessarily mean the complete severance of tangible ties between men on earth and their companions who are no longer here.

Before passing on to a more important subject, may I say a few words on the question of attempting to communicate with intelligences in the invisible realms around us. We are in the midst of an upheaval greater than any previous experience in human history. The effects of this upheaval (and possibly some of its causes also) are to be perceived in that borderland state into which we pass at death. This is a time for prayer and silence rather than for attempts to open doorways of communication between those who are in different states of consciousness, whether through the agency of automatism or trance. There is considerable danger that forces of a chaotic and mischievous character may be unwittingly released through the unwise opening of such avenues, with results that can but prove deplorable. Communion of a spiritual character between mind and mind through the agency of trained or natural clairvoyance falls into another category and may prove of service during these times of tribulation.

Finally there is a matter of great moment about which I should like to say something.

We have seers in our midst who can look far beyond human horizons and whose vision can be of immense service at the present time. This vision contains what may be called a prophetic element, but as this is of universal rather than of personal application, value can, I think, be attached to it. These seers report the gradual approach towards human levels of a wave of illumination and spiritual power emanating from higher regions beyond the ken of most of us. They report the coming of a greater Light than has yet pierced the darkness in which we live. There may be a few present here today who will remember that this approaching Event was touched upon when I spoke in this hall some fifteen years ago, and has indeed been referred to by more than one speaker or visionary at intervals during the past half-century. In spite of the two world wars and the uneasy peace which separated them, the radiance thrown out by this coming Illumination has continued to grow in strength and imminency. It is, I believe, within the power of the human race to accelerate or retard the momentum of a revelation that will ultimately uplift life upon this planet and in the intermediary worlds as well to an extent that at present seems incredible. Each one is asked to prepare himself as a channel for receiving and passing on this illumination. It contains a Divine leaven through which humanity may be purified, uplifted and transfigured.

Rightly directed, there is a greater power in the exercise of *Expectation* than is generally realised. We are asked to *expect* in faith the coming of a new dawn for the human race and to begin to reflect the light of this dawn within our hearts and minds. The actual form in which this Coming may show itself objectively is a matter of secondary importance, and need not unduly concern us now, but it seems evident that the recognition of the creative Presence in and around us as a living reality will help to speed that advent which we have been told to expect.

It does seem important to remember that light, love and wisdom are the birthright of every son of the Father and that illumination must first be reflected within the individual and then be sent out in all directions from each such centre of life and being.

Surely it is your and my duty and privilege to so discipline and train ourselves in silence and through the stilling of the self that we may become servitors of value in the drama now unfolding. How few there are who have begun to understand the power of Silence! Stillness begets awareness of spiritual realities as an interior and personal experience which can come in no other way. The complete stilling of the self would seem to be the doorway through which the Christ revelation for the new age may come in and dwell with us . . . dwell with each awakening man and woman, and in so dwelling bring that peace which must precede the descent of the Kingdom into our midst.

Chapter Five

Psychic Methods of Reception

THE HOUSEKEEPER TO a Quaker lady friend of mine was in the habit of coming down to breakfast each morning and then quoting from memory teaching which had been given to her during the silence of sleep. Her mistress made a record of these quotations and ultimately sent the script to me. Apart from the faulty grammar and the excessive length of sentences, there was little to criticise in a literary sense, and the teaching itself showed inspiration of a high order. After the necessary revisions had been made, this record was published under the title *Christ in You** being financed by a Scotsman who was a close friend of mine. This inspiring little book has run into many editions, here, in America and in Europe, and it continues to meet a steady demand. This is the first time that its origin has been disclosed, the book having been published anonymously. When sleep is preceded by the stilling of the mind and by prayer, the results can prove of untold value, especially if those concerned have learnt how to retain in memory the impressions received whilst the body and the brain are quiescent.

It is not unusual for problems that have proved

* *Christ in You* (J. M. Watkins, London).

intractable during waking hours to be solved quite naturally whilst the body and the brain are asleep.

The Dangers of Psychic Automatism

Elsewhere in these notes I refer to the dangers and uncertainties connected with the use of artificial methods for obtaining information on 'other-worldly' matters. In taking this view I have no wish to suggest that nothing of value or interest results from the use of these agencies. Spiritualistic literature covers a wide range, including useful teaching on philosophical and metaphysical subjects. To dismiss all these 'communications' as valueless would be both presumptuous and untrue. However, in regard to the information provided in this way about conditions on the other side of 'death', one fact stands out, and it should not be ignored. There appears to be no agreement between those who 'communicate' in this way. Statements about the future life and how it is lived are so contradictory that it is difficult to find among them any common ground. For this reason, to accept them as a reliable guide would seem to be unwise. I think it fair to consider seriously whether as the result of the large number of 'spirit' communications received during the past half-century we are today any nearer definite proof of the *permanent* survival of the individual or are in possession of accurate details relating to the conditions of such survival?

Communications of this sort have without doubt brought comfort and consolation to many thousands of those in distress and sorrow. To deny them such satisfaction would be cruel, but surely the time has come to replace the artificial and automatic methods still so prevalent by the more evolutionary agencies through which natural clairvoyance and the training of the mind can be used in order to differentiate between the brain's imagining and true inner vision?

I would include trance mediumship among the artificial methods referred to above, but in saying this I do not wish to cause offence. In my experience the great majority of those who practise this profession are men and women of high character and ideals. Voluntarily and with the best of motives they allow their minds and bodies to be invaded by disembodied entities, over whose activities they have no control. They are willing to stand aside in order to be used as channels of communication with another world of life and being. By doing so they feel that they are fulfilling a valuable mission, undertaken with good motives and for the purpose of bringing enlightenment to those who seek their help. However, the dangers involved in the process of what might be called automatic possession are rarely recognised, nor the fact that such practices are devolutionary in character rather then progressive.

In the long run, certainty as to whether the gift of eternal life belongs to each one of us or not will never be obtained from sources outside ourselves. Certainty comes from within and can never reach us in any other way. Prayer and Silence are the gateways through which such certainty can be reached, and meanwhile simple, confident faith can prove a most valuable stepping-stone towards certitude. Children 'enter in' because they are not dominated by the pride of the intellect, which stumbling-block can prove so dangerous to those of maturer years. There can be no final or finite proof of immortality short of immortality itself.

An Observer on the 'Other Side'

Let us now consider the conditions likely to be met with immediately after physical death has taken place, viewed from the standpoint of an observer.

Physical death is as natural a process as that of birth and in some ways it is similar in operation. Nine months is spent in the mother's womb in the preparation of a body for use during life on earth. A new-born babe possesses in embryo all those faculties that are to develop gradually for his use in later life. Sometimes an individual comes into 'full possession of his faculties', as the saying is, by the time he is seven years old. At the other extreme there are those who never appear to reach maturity at any period in their lives. Usually a man's mental and emotional faculties emerge naturally as his body grows into full stature. In some instances a point is reached when the further development of these faculties appears to cease, to become static. In other cases the process continues throughout life and well into a mellow age. So much the better.

When we are born into the next world, the order of events is very similar. Almost invariably there is a period of sleep, which state can be likened to the period spent in a mother's womb. When awakening takes place the new arrival gradually becomes conscious of the fact that he is still alive and still in possession of everything that made him a conscious and living entity on earth. The absence of a physical body proves to be of no inconvenience, because the new arrival discovers that it has been replaced by a 'fresh' and much more adaptable 'form' now ready for his use. Just as a baby has to learn how to use his arms and legs, how gradually to control his bodily activities, so does a similar process take place when one is born into the next world. It is a fascinating experience, because the new body or form is capable of a far wider range of interesting activities than was the case in connection with the body he has left behind him.

The new arrival soon discovers with surprise that each time he thinks a thought, or feels an emotion, these thoughts and emotions at once assume appearances of their own and surround him as tangible realities. He then begins to learn how to direct and control his thinking and his feeling in order not to be overwhelmed by a complexity of dominating 'bodyguards'. It is, of course, impossible to put into language a description of these conditions which would bring understanding to the majority of those who have not yet experienced them. The new arrival slowly recovers memory of his previous existence, a memory which in time throws off much dross, but still retains in a distilled form the important elements which make memory such a wonderful possession.

A 'time' comes, if one dare use the word, when the individual whose experiences we are describing discovers that he need not stay in one 'place', but can move about at will as freely and fully as he so desires. This discovery brings a sense of amazement and joy. He begins to explore his strange and often interesting surroundings and then becomes conscious of the presence of other beings, similarly placed, with whom he can 'converse' in a manner that might be called telepathic for lack of a word giving a more accurate definition of the process. As memory becomes more active, recollection of his past life grows stronger, and this is often accompanied by a desire to return into the conditions he was used to before he 'died'.

At this stage of the process I am describing it is usual for the new arrival to see before him a panoramic picture or review of the main events and experiences which made up his life on earth. This strange and arresting phenomenon may give pleasure or sorrow, happiness or regret. What is called Purgatory often consists in the bitter recollections resulting from the vision of a misspent or evil life lived out on earth. It is too late now to remedy one's sins, to rectify cruelties and injustices for which one may have been responsible. Remorse can create a state of depression and anxiety which in itself is a form of Hell. It should be remembered that the thoughts and feelings engendered at such a time immediately take an outward form of their own and surround their victim so that he feels imprisoned and deprived of all initiative. Although a wise man once said that 'Regret is the lowest use to which memory can be put' we should not forget that remorse for wrongdoing, for selfish and sensual actions, for the abuse of the gift of life, can be both terrible and salutary.

It is not long after the new arrival recovers consciousness and memory that he begins to experience what one may call a two-way 'gravitational pull'. Here again we lack a word that will describe accurately the meaning of this term. He feels the presence of an attraction back towards the earthly conditions he has so recently left behind him. On the other hand, there seems to be present an upward pull, one capable of lifting him out of his strange and often difficult surroundings towards a more harmonious level of consciousness and action. This two-way gravitational pull can be extremely unpleasant and often continues for a period which seems unendurable in length. One who leaves earth unprepared to do so, entrenched mentally in the love of sensuous and sensual pleasures, now finds himself attracted almost intolerably back to those material conditions from which he departed so reluctantly.

Then, of course, there is the natural desire of those who have left their loved ones behind to return to them and to relive experiences of which they now find themselves deprived. It is all very puzzling and difficult, but useful lessons are being learnt and in due course it will be realised that progress upward is the law, which law can only be ignored at one's peril.

Now let us look at the prospect as it appears to those who have been left behind, mourning their departed relatives or friends, uncertain perhaps as to the fate which may have overtaken them. What can be more natural than the desire to contact and even bring back into communication these loved ones who have gone before? Whilst this desire is the inevitable result of grief, it can prove very selfish and may harm the loved one more deeply than is realised. The task of those on earth should be to lift consciousness, through prayer and silence, to a level where natural communion can be achieved. There is great danger in reversing this process by trying to pull back the person concerned into earthly conditions.

Many of those who are distracted by their grief seek the services of mediums to act as intermediaries. Or they experiment with automatic writing and similar devices. In these ways the gravitational pull downwards is intensified and progress for the departed one in his efforts to escape from the intermediary realm towards a higher and happier level is obstructed and often delayed indefinitely. To give way to the temptation of trying to return to earth levels is both dangerous and devolutionary. For those of us still on earth who co-operate in this endeavour, whether from selfish or personal motives, the penalty may prove severe.

It should also be remembered that conditions in what we have called the intermediary or borderland realm are rendered confused and discordant as a result of the struggle to respond to the downward gravitational pull. The attitude of mind and the practices referred to above may result in those we love being obliged to remain in that region between earth and Heaven, to use conventional language, far longer and more miserably than is necessary. Also, their effect upon so many who are striving to rise out of purgatorial conditions is serious, making it far more difficult for them to resist the lure to turn backwards towards that material state which is their habitation no longer.

PSYCHIC METHODS OF RECEPTION

As we have been dealing with the conditions likely to be met in Borderland, it may not be amiss to add a note on sudden death and its effects.

In this connection, I cannot do better than quote the experiences of a soldier killed in battle during the first world war. Confirmation of what he told me, within a few weeks of his passing, has come to hand from many other sources since. For this reason confidence can be placed, I think, in the validity of what follows. I will quote the ideas expressed by my soldier friend in words which are as exact an interpretation of his meaning as is possible.

On a Monday in March 1917 whilst I was home on leave I happened to be walking along the sands at Bournemouth when I felt the presence of someone behind me and I heard steps and these followed me for the rest of the day. Suddenly I found myself saying to myself, 'It is a soldier who has been killed in battle who wants to make his presence known.' The steps were followed by a voice and finally by a presence and the following is a record, taken down at the time, of the message 'Private Dowding' was so anxious to impart:

> My name is of no importance; apparently names over here are not needed. I became a soldier in the autumn of 1915, and left my narrow village life behind. I joined as a private and died as a private. My soldiering lasted just nine months, eight of which were spent training in Northumberland. I went out with my battalion to France in July 1916, and we went into the trenches almost at once. I was killed by a shell splinter one evening in August, and I believe that my body was buried the following day. As you see, I hasten over these unimportant events, important to me once, but now of no real consequence. How we overestimate the significance of earthly happenings! One only realises this when freed from earthly ties.
>
> Well, my body soon became cannon fodder, and there were few to mourn me. It was not for me to play anything

but an insignificant part in this world—tragedy, which is still unfolding.

I am still myself, a person of no importance; but I feel I should like to say a few things before passing along. I feared death, but then that was natural. I was timid, and even feared life and its pitfalls. So I was afraid of being killed and was sure it would mean extinction. There are still many who believe this. It is because extinction has not come to me that I want to speak to you. May I describe my experiences? Perhaps they may prove useful to you. How necessary that some of us should speak back across the border! The barriers must be broken down. This is one of the ways of doing it. Listen therefore to what I have to say.

Physical death is nothing. There really is no cause for fear. Some of my pals grieved for me. When I 'went west' they thought I was dead for good. This is what happened. I have a perfectly clear memory of the whole incident. I was waiting at the corner of a traverse to go on guard. It was a fine evening. I had no special intimation of danger, until I heard the whizz of a shell. Then followed an explosion somewhere behind me. I crouched down involuntarily, but was too late. Something struck, hard, hard, hard, against my neck. Shall I ever lose the memory of that hardness? It is the only unpleasant incident that I can remember. I fell, and as I did so, without passing through any apparent interval of unconsciousness, I found myself outside myself! You see I am telling my story simply; you will find it easier to understand. You will learn to know what a small incident this dying is. Think of it! One moment I was alive, in the earthly sense, looking over a trench parapet, unalarmed, normal. Five seconds later I was standing outside my body, helping two of my pals to carry my body down the trench labyrinth towards a dressing station. They thought I was senseless but alive. I did not know whether I had jumped out of my body through shell shock, temporarily or for ever. You see what a small thing is death, even the violent death of war! I seemed in a dream! I had dreamt that some-one or something had knocked me down. Now I was dreaming that I was outside my body. Soon I should wake up and find myself in the traverse waiting to go on guard.

... It all happened so simply. Death for me was a simple experience—no horror, no long-drawn suffering, no conflict. It comes to many in the same way. My pals need not fear death. Few of them do; nevertheless, there is an underlying dread of possible extinction. I dreaded that; many soldiers do, but they rarely have time to think about such things. As in my case, thousands of soldiers pass over without knowing it. If there be shock, it is not the shock of physical death. Shock comes later when comprehension dawns: 'Where is my body? Surely I am not dead!' In my own case I knew nothing more than I have already related, at the time. When I found that my two pals could carry my body without my help, I dropped behind; I just followed, in a curiously humble way. Humble? Yes, because I seemed so useless. We met a stretcher party. My body was hoisted on to the stretcher. I wondered when I should get back into it again. You see, I was so little 'dead' that I imagined I was still (physically) alive. Think of it a moment before we pass on. I had been struck by a shell splinter. There was no pain. The life was knocked out of my body; again I say there was no pain. Then I found that the whole of myself—all, that is, that thinks and sees and feels and knows—was still alive and conscious. I will tell you what I felt like. It was as if I had been running hard until, hot and breathless, I had thrown my overcoat away. The coat was my body, and if I had not thrown it away I should have been suffocated. I cannot describe the experience any better way; there is nothing else to describe.

My body went to the first dressing station, and after examination was taken to a mortuary. I stayed near it all that night, watching, but without thoughts. It was as if my being, feeling and thinking had become suspended by some Power outside myself. This sensation came over me gradually as the night advanced. I still expected to wake up in my body again—that is, so far as I expected anything. Then I lost consciousness and slept soundly.

. . . . .

No detail seems to have escaped me. When I awoke my body had disappeared! How I hunted and hunted! It began to dawn upon me that something strange had happened, although I still felt I was in a dream and should soon awake. My body had been buried or burned; I never knew which. Soon I ceased hunting for it. Then the shock came! It came without any warning, suddenly. I had been killed by a German shell! I was dead! I was no longer alive. I had been killed, killed, killed! Curious that I felt no shock when I was first driven outside my body. Now the shock came, and it was very real. I tried to think backwards but my memory was numb. (It returned later.) How does it feel to be 'dead'? One can't explain because there's nothing in it! I simply felt free and light. My being seemed to have expanded. These are mere words. I can only tell you just this: that death is nothing unseemly or shocking. So simple is the 'passing along' experience that it beggars description. Others may have other experiences to relate of a more complex nature. I don't know....

Let me relate my first experience after I had somewhat recovered from the shock of realising I was 'dead'.

I was on, or rather above, the battlefield. It seemed as if I were floating in a mist that muffled sound and blurred the vision. Through this mist slowly penetrated a dim picture and some very low sounds. It was like looking through the wrong end of a telescope. Everything was distant, minute, misty, unreal. Guns were being fired. It might all have been millions of miles away. The detonation hardly reached me; I was conscious of the shells bursting without actually seeing them. The ground seemed very empty. No soldiers were visible. It was like looking down from above the clouds, yet that doesn't exactly express it either. When a shell that took life exploded then the sensation of it came much nearer to me. The noise and tumult came over the border-line with the lives of the slain. A curious way of putting it. All this time I was very lonely. I was conscious of no one near me. I was neither in the world of matter nor could I be sure I was in any place at all! Just simply conscious of my own existence in a state of dream. I think I fell asleep for the second time, and long remained unconscious and in a dreamless condition.

. . . . .

PSYCHIC METHODS OF RECEPTION

At last I awoke. Then a new sensation came to me. It was as if I stood on a pinnacle, all that was essential of me. The rest receded, receded, receded. All appertaining to bodily life seemed to be dropping away down into a bottomless abyss. There was no feeling of irretrievable loss. My being seemed both minute and expansive at the same time. All that was not really me slipped down and away. The sense of loneliness deepened.

. . . . .

I do not find it easy to express myself. If the ideas are not clear, that is not your fault. You are setting down just what I impress upon you. How do I know this? I cannot see your pen, but I see my ideas as they are caught up and whirled into form within your mind. By 'form' perhaps I mean words. Others may not feel this loneliness. I cannot tell whether my experiences are common to many in a like position. When I first 'awoke' the second time I felt cramped. This is passing and a sense of real freedom comes over me. A load has dropped away from me. I think my new faculties are now in working order. I can reason and think and feel and move.

I am simply myself, alive, in a region where food and drink seem unnecessary. Otherwise 'life' is strangely similar to earth life. A 'continuation' but with more freedom. I have no more to say just now.

Thank you for listening to me.*

It is only right to add here that the passing-out experience is not always so easy as in Private Dowding's case. When the emotions of fear or hatred are uppermost the transition can be far more difficult. For the consolation of those who have lost their loved ones in war or as the result of accident, the following fact should be recorded.

There exist in the Borderland region a number of groups and organisations similar in function to our Red Cross Societies on earth. Their members are drawn

* *Private Dowding* by W. T. P. (J. M. Watkins, London).

from those who have been specially trained in what might be termed rescue work.

These important activities are undertaken by volunteers, many of whom were alive on earth not so long ago. They are equipped with hospitals, rest houses and educational centres on a scale adequate to meet all urgent needs.

It has been my privilege on many occasions to take part in these 'life-saving' activities. Those readers who believe in prayer should remember these devoted helpers and their healing ministry.

The time may come when many of us will be only too glad to avail ourselves of the services of these selfless and dedicated beings.

Building for the Future

It is easy to believe that we stand where we do in life as the result of circumstances over which we have had no control. Nothing can be farther from the truth. The house I live in, my friends, my general surroundings, in fact all the circumstances of my life are not the outcome of fortuitous events. On the contrary, it is my thoughts and actions in the past which are solely responsible for what I am today and for the conditions which surround me now.

We cannot evade the effects of causes which we have originated in the past. To this extent we are the slaves of our yesterdays but can become the masters of our tomorrows.

The working of the law of cause and effect does not cease when we pass out of our present world. At this very moment you and I are fashioning the circumstances and conditions which are destined to surround us on the other side of 'death'. Here and now we are building the habitations we shall occupy there and the circumstances of our environment.

Using the language of symbols, my present thoughts and actions are the bricks and mortar from which my future home will be built. It is within your and my power to prepare our habitations and our surroundings for good or ill in the realm which awaits us beyond the veil.

I would suggest that you do not dismiss this conception as being too far-fetched for thoughtful consideration. Through the use of prayer, constructive thinking and right actions here and now, let us use the gift of true imagination to begin the construction of a lovely house and garden for use in the hereafter, a place of harmony and light suitable to enable us to carry on our lives in happiness and service. Let us learn how to become the masters of our tomorrows.

Whether you agree with me or not, one fact cannot be evaded. The law that governs human welfare never ceases to operate but, being based on love and justice, it can be our best friend when obeyed but our worst enemy when we try to disregard and flout it.

Communion and Communication

Let us now consider how we can best help forward on their upward way those who have left us temporarily behind.

After all, it will not be long before we ourselves must face the same problems and the same temptations. The first lesson to be mastered is to learn how to release from the bondage of our thinking those whom we so strongly desire should return to our earth in order to make their tangible presence seen and felt. Communion rather than communication is surely the goal for which we should strive. By communion I mean our capacity to lift consciousness to a point where mind can meet mind without the need to draw those we love back into mundane conditions. 'The Communion of Saints' is no empty phrase. It is a communion available to us as well, although we have not yet attained the qualities of sainthood. Communion is in itself a form of communication, far removed from the region of words, yet completely satisfying in itself. The contact is direct between mind and mind, no intermediary being necessary. The experiences recorded in this book have not involved the employment of a third party as a transmitting agent.

There is nothing artificial or automatic in the process, which is both a natural and a spiritual one.

The universal Mind in which all living beings dwell need not be divided arbitrarily into watertight compartments, each being cut off from the rest. In this Mind which is our eternal habitation we can learn how to move forward freely, yes even whilst still seemingly confined within the trammels of the flesh.

The dedicated use of prayer and silence is the surest means for enabling us to commune with saints and angels, and to do so with those who have already departed from this life and with whom the bond of love is strong and enduring. This is the ideal we should set before us rather than the use of artificial forms of communication of a kind which obstruct and delay the upward progress of those no longer with us. Words are too feeble to make transcendental ideas of this kind easily understood or available for our practical use here and now. Revelation is an interior process and neither you nor I can attain it from books or people or from other external sources.

> The piercing of the veils must come about through spiritual and natural processes of mind and heart, and not through the employment of magic, ritual or trance.*

> * ('The Messenger'—as quoted in *Private Dowding*)

Chapter Six

The Enigma of Sex

NOW I TURN to a subject which involves treading on delicate ground. First let me make it clear that I claim no authority for anything I write and that it is not my wish to seek either acceptance or rejection for the views put forward. We are all novices in matters spiritual and at best can only hope to be used as channels through whom a glimpse of understanding may be allowed to flow.

I have already touched upon certain similarities between the process of being born into this world and being born into the next. The use of the word 'procreation' tends to give many people the idea that the physical union of a man and a woman is capable of producing a new life, an entirely virgin entity now coming into existence for the first time. That the spirit, mind and soul belonging to a new-born babe have enjoyed a previous existence is unacceptable to many parents, who, on the other hand, believe that they themselves are solely responsible for the creative act. Those who are more thoughtful will have realised the truth that God is the only Creator and that the men and women He has created, whilst capable of reproducing form in matter, cannot create the life and intelligence inhabiting the form which results from sexual union.

Far too many parents regard the children they bring into this world as their personal property, little above the level of their other goods and chattels. They tend to consider their offspring as their property and not as their trustees. 'My child belongs to me and to my husband and to no one else.' This and similar remarks to the same effect are all too common. Such an attitude may not be intended to be taken literally, but the inference is there too often to be ignored as resulting from mere thoughtlessness.

A minority in the modern world still look upon marriage as a divine sacrament, a dedicated alliance of a man and woman for mutual companionship and for the fulfilment of fore-ordained purposes of great evolutionary import, purposes which may or may not result in conception in outward form. Others look upon the marriage ceremony, whether taking place in church or in a registrar's office, solely as a means for legalising cohabitation, and with no other important purpose in view. This statement may sound exaggerated, but it certainly contains an element of truth. The provision of a suitable form for the use of an immortal soul awaiting entry into this world to fulfil purposes of moment is such an important task that to undertake it lightly is little short of blasphemy. Far too often sexual intercourse is looked upon as a pleasant but transitory indulgence, one that is a sufficient end in itself. Many children, as a result, are brought into this world by accident rather than by design. Can there be any object in setting down these well-known facts? Consideration of some of the deeper aspects of the subject may prove useful, even if the only result is to give the opportunity for a few of those whom it concerns intimately to pause and think and think again.

Each time that, as a result of sexual intercourse, the

life essences, male and female, are blended, something important happens. This is true whether the act is undertaken casually or with serious intent. A certain energy of etheric potency is released containing an instinctive life of its own, irrespective of whether procreation in an external sense results or not. To release such an energy for no other purpose than to gratify a sensual desire cannot be the fulfilment of a Divine law, though it appears to satisfy an urge which is felt to be both natural and desirable. Even on the human plane there is a sanctity connected with the release of a force which contains within itself a specific potentiality which may result in the sowing of a seed designed by Nature's alchemy to become a human habitation. Words are powerless to explain clearly the seen and unseen effects produced when the sexual act is consummated. These effects are by no means confined to the two participants. The unseen outflow resulting from the generative process radiates widely. Its influence for good or ill is not lessened by the fact that its effects do not show themselves externally in a manner that can be seen and measured. Whenever the sexual union takes place as a purely sensual rather than as a sacramental act, the influences or energies released cannot find employment in beneficial ways and may do great and widespread harm. It is unlikely that many readers will treat the above assertion seriously. They will think that its implications are too far-fetched and that they make no concession to human frailties. I cannot quarrel with them if they do, because no words are available to provide an acceptable explanation of what has just been said.

It would take a book even to begin to explain the bases and the reasons for the views I have expressed. Here again is a region of knowledge and understanding that cannot be imparted by one person to another. Such knowledge and the understanding behind it can only be obtained intuitively by those who are ready to receive and willing to act upon it. If, however, we descend from the speculative heights to the level of eugenics, here is an issue that should be faced and treated seriously.

Is it not strange and very wrong that the human race in general should devote more care and skill to the breeding of its animals and pets than to the propagation of its own species? How can we expect to attract into incarnation souls of pure and high qualities, souls whose presence in our midst would prove of incalculable benefit, if we are unwilling to provide them with bodies that are conceived under the best possible physical, psychic and mental conditions? With this very pertinent question offered for your consideration, I will leave the subject, only regretting my inability to place it before you in a more adequate and convincing way.

CHAPTER SEVEN

The Attitude of the Sceptic

THE NOTES WHICH form the basis for this book were shown, before publication, to a scientific friend who would describe himself in matters of this kind as an 'honest but open-minded sceptic'. This description seems to involve a contradiction in terms, but let that pass. His attitude can be summed up as follows: 'I approach the study of all phenomena incapable of scientific proof with curiosity but also with a considerable measure of suspicion.' Recently this scientist made what he described as being a detailed and objective investigation into the evidence so far produced in connection with the apparitions known as flying saucers. His verdict in this connection was 'Not proven'

I asked this friend to set down frankly his comments on the experiences that I am sharing with you now I thought it would be interesting to discover whether any common ground existed between his outlook and my own. Here is what he wrote, which he sent me on the understanding that his name and standing should not be disclosed.

> I have read your notes with interest and with some amusement. Thank you for showing them to me. The range

of your experiences is quite remarkable, but I could find in them no evidence that could be subjected to scientific proof. Frankly, in my view, some of the stories you relate are so incredible that they lead me to the conclusion that your forthcoming book is intended to be a work of fiction and not a serious contribution to human knowledge. You seem to evade any opportunity to equate the information you present with the vast range of phenomena already known to science and for which reasonable proof has been deduced and accepted as such by the scientific world of today. Therefore I feel unable to offer you any useful comments.

In writing to thank my friend for giving me his views, I told him that had I been briefed as counsel for the prosecution the case I could have presented would, in my view, have been far more convincing and logical than his own. It was my hope that this rejoinder would draw him out and that, as a result, some common ground between us might have been discovered. To date, however, no further word has come from him, which seems a pity.

Let us examine what he says: The reference to 'scientific proof' is interesting. This term, I take it, is intended to apply to all phenomena that can be shown to obey the laws of science and of physics to the extent that these are known and generally accepted *at the present time*. These laws, I understand, apply strictly and solely to our three-dimensional world of matter. If this statement is untrue, I willingly stand to be corrected.

The extent to which the laws of physics can be applied to experiences taking place within the mind of man is surely a very open question? Would it not be true to say that the rule of scientific law as known today cannot be applied usefully to the realm of such experiences as those with which this book is dealing? No yardstick seems to exist at our present stage of knowledge which can be used for measuring the relations between the world of matter and the world of mind. Here again I stand open to correction. Were not my friend so famous in his own field, I might venture to comment on his use of the word 'incredible' as being unscientific in its implications. Every discovery made by man has seemed to be incredible to the orthodox thinkers of the day. As a recent example one could cite the way in which Einstein was pilloried by his fellow scientists when first he made his revolutionary discoveries known. Surely the word 'incredible' should be deleted from the scientific dictionary?

My friend goes on to liken what I have written to a 'work of fiction'. Before making this comparison it might have been well to pause and think awhile. The conversion of much once believed to be fiction into fact is an unending process, never truer than at the present time. Open-minded enquirers should surely be willing to agree that no defining line can be drawn between fact and fiction, and by fiction in this instance I wish to confine its application to the kind of experiences related in this book.

My friendly critic then goes on to suggest that I have made no effort to 'equate the information you present with the vast range of phenomena already known to science and for which reasonable proof has been deduced, and accepted as such by the scientific world of today'. I find this a very surprising statement. Use of the word 'today', to my way of thinking, undermines the value of what in my case I should regard as an unscientific and incorrect assertion.

The range of human knowledge never ceases to unroll and to expand. The incredibilities of yesterday are continually being converted into the facts of today, and here I am using the word 'fact' in the same sense as my critic has applied to it. It should also be remembered with due humility that many so-called scientific facts of yesterday have now been relegated to the realm of fiction. Based on the reasons he has given, my critic reaches the conclusion that 'he cannot offer any useful comments'. Earlier in his statement he had accused me of evasion, and, in the light of the above remark, I see no reason why I should not return the compliment.

For the peace of mind of those who like my friend would question the validity of my outlook and of the experiences I have set down, let me emphasise what has already been written earlier. I am no propagandist. I do not seek a verdict of 'Guilty' or 'Not guilty' for the truth or falsity of the narratives this book contains. It would be most surprising if their truth were to be accepted in the light of the findings and conclusions of the material science of today. Indeed I am prepared to go further by confessing that I myself am doubtful as to whether what are recognised as facts today, and what is currently regarded as fiction, can be clearly separated one from the other. The passage of time is on the side of those who seek for the truth honestly, interiorly, and with open minds.

The Closed Mind

One of the most alarming features of modern times is the widespread growth of the conviction that the human intellect at its so-called best is an all-sufficient guide to life and action. May I cite a case in point?

For some years past I have followed closely the various brains trust programmes that have become so popular a feature on radio and television. Those who are asked to take part in these stimulating discussions are selected carefully from leaders of thought drawn from scientific, educational and literary circles. In this way it is evidently felt that the cream of the instructed thinking of today is made available to many millions of viewers at the same time. Usually as a result we are treated to a brilliant exhibition of the all-consuming pride of the human intellect in its self-sufficiency.

Generalities are dangerous and I apologise to those to whom the above criticism does not apply. One wonders whether the producers of these programmes ever stop to consider seriously their responsibilities to the public, a public quite unable to make its own views heard? From time to time questions are discussed dealing with problems of human survival, religious beliefs and what may be termed loosely 'other-worldly matters'. On such occasions one notices a certain freezing of the atmosphere, a drawing-in of horns. What is still more surprising is the fact that a majority of the speakers (and I use the word 'majority' with care) seem over-ready to declare their unbelief in the continuation of human existence beyond the confines of our present life on earth. Some of the most brilliant of these intellectual giants appear to glory in labelling themselves agnostics and in the fact that they refuse to allow their intellects to be trammelled by the 'shackles' of religion in any form. Let me quote a case in point in order that I may not be accused of exaggeration.

On a recent occasion a panel of distinguished thinkers was asked to discuss the relation between fact and illusion. No serious attempt was made to define the meaning of these words or to consider that the intellect unaided is by no means competent to differentiate between the two. As I have written elsewhere, many so-called 'facts' accepted as true by one generation are relegated to the realm of fiction by the next, and vice versa. It happens in almost every field of human knowledge that fact and fiction are liable to change places with bewildering frequency.

Any serious student of the history of physics, for example, will find himself bound to accept the validity of the above assertion. It is true that we are now living in what is called an age of materialism, a period during which experiences beyond the understanding of the intellect are regarded with scornful scepticism. Here again is a generalisation, which while containing an important element of truth should be regarded warily. Dogmatism in matters spiritual can be as dangerous as belief in the infallibility of the reasoning power of the human brain.

On the occasion to which I have just referred, one of the speakers, a person of undoubted intellectual standing, made a statement so remarkable that I cannot refrain from comment. Whilst accepting the prevalent definition of illusion as being something which is contrary to 'fact' and therefore 'untrue', he went on to explain his view that illusions were valuable and indeed essential to happiness and peace of mind. When challenged he cited, as an example, the fact that he knew the Biblical story of Creation, and much else recorded in the Jewish and Christian Scriptures, was illusory and untrue; nevertheless, he said that he felt no inconsistency in accepting what he knew to be false and contrary to reason! Two of the other speakers lost no time in voicing their dissent, being careful to make it clear that nothing could be true for them which was incapable of being proved through the exercise of reason and common sense.

Reason and common sense? Here are the venerated watchwords of those who rely implicitly upon the much-vaunted supremacy of the human animal's capacity to decide between what is 'true' and what is 'false'. I have heard a statement to the following effect put forward recently more than once, 'Modern thought has now outgrown the need to believe in God and in an after life'. Pride in the self-sufficiency of the intellect could hardly be carried further.

On several occasions I have challenged in private one or other of these leaders of modern thought, intellectual giants in their own field. I have told them that in my view they are suffering from the trammels of a closed mind. The fat is then well and truly in the fire. I am assured that nothing could be further from the truth, that my criticism is both unjust and incorrect. In one such instance I purposely went out of my way to relate an 'other-worldly' experience of my own, similar in content to those which are included in this book. It was fascinating to watch the process by which my listener set to work to close his mind and to refuse even a passing doubt to cloud his reasoning power.—'What have I to do with the fantasies of a mind deranged?'—This thought may not have been expressed in words, but the inference was plain to see.

It is alarming to reflect that our modern system of education is to a large extent devised and carried out by men and women whose minds appear to be closed in this way.

The influence of scientific thought and reasoning leaves little room for a reverent consideration of religion and its claims. Reason so dominates faith that the latter has come to be regarded as the plaything of the weak and thoughtless. Here, of course, I am speaking of a subtle and pervasive trend, one that at present is almost paramount in its influence upon the young. What a shock awaits these prisoners of their own minds when the time comes for them to stand naked and dismayed outside their prison houses! That time must come inevitably for one and all, and cannot be evaded. The state of Purgatory can be a fearful experience for many whose attitude of mind whilst still on earth is similar to the examples I have given. Do not dismiss my words lightly even if it may have been necessary to exaggerate my thesis, in order to drive home an important truth. A little child who accepts the fact that 'I of myself can do nothing' is nearer the gates of Heaven than those who assert that 'I of myself [unaided] can do and know everything that is worth doing and knowing'.

The virtue of humility is sadly conspicuous by its absence in the thinking processes of so many leaders in our modern civilisation.

The notion that a 'little child shall lead them' is far too often dismissed out of hand as being contrary to reason and common sense.

In saying this I shall be accused of the very evil of dogmatic statement which I so deplore and as underestimating the value of the use of the human intelligence in many useful fields of life and action. How difficult it is to state a case fairly without lapsing into generalities, which can be both sweeping and unfair! I have spoken of the trend towards belief in the infallibility of that form of intellectual reasoning which has assumed Godlike proportions in these so-called 'progressive' days. Fortunately there is another and more inspiring side to the picture.

'Closed minds' can open. Realisation can dawn that the capacities of the brain are limited and cannot be regarded as infallible agencies through which understanding can be reached. Even during my own lifetime it has been possible to witness a decided trend towards a larger measure of open-mindedness, a trend which in time must reach and influence the most entrenched exponents of the materialistic outlook. I will hazard the guess that whereas half a century ago impartial consideration of the experiences I am now sharing with you would have been dismissed as fiction, today there are signs of a willingness to listen to thoughts that may not be understood, but which are now beginning to receive serious consideration. Someone has said that the seeming lunatics of one generation have been known to become the wise men of the next, and, in part, history is on the side of this assertion. In this connection Shakespeare has voiced the truth in one of his wisest sayings. I can well believe that he was a man of humility, a genius who fully recognised the limitations of the intellect, unaided.

It is the 'closed mind' which is largely responsible for having brought the human race to the very brink of disaster, to a point where the pressing of a button can result in man's extinction overnight. If you think carefully it will be clear to you that there is no exaggeration in this statement. Surely it is the fruit of intellectual pride that has resulted in men's gross and impertinent interference with the fundamental processes of Nature and with the cosmic rhythm of our planet, upon which so much depends? Recently I mentioned this idea to a leading scientist in the realm of atomic research. To my surprise his response was quite untypical of what one might expect from such a quarter. I cannot reveal his identity; great men are naturally more jealous of their reputations than we lesser mortals. They are fearful of one another's criticisms. This is what he said in regard to the atomic problem:

'We are playing with forces that are not yet under our control and so far we understand little about them. Some of us realise that we are in process of releasing energies which may assume mastery over us. It is too late now to retrace our steps and to take another path. We must go on. It is my hope, not a very strong one, that in time to avert disaster we may discover means for harnessing the energies we have so recently released and begin to understand what we have done and why we have done it. In any case we must go on, ready to accept whatever consequences may follow.'

I asked this learned and famous man whether he did not feel that the time had come to seek spiritual guidance in matters of such devastating importance to the human race? For a while he looked at me uncomprehendingly with an expression of amazement. Then he replied to my question with passion and sincerity. And what he said was this: 'For God's sake, show us how.'

. . . .

(It is strange how often those who call themselves atheists will invoke the name of God when faced by some problem or crisis beyond their understanding.)

It is wonderful to watch the gradual opening of a mind hitherto closed to a consideration of spiritual realities.

When I spoke of prayer as one of the sure gateways to understanding, he did not dismiss the notion out of hand. He told me that the capacity to pray aright and with prospect of results involved laws beyond the range of scientific knowledge. Maybe (he thought) to tamper with such laws in ignorance might result in dangers as great as those which have resulted from interference with the laws of Nature. However, I left him in what I could see was a very thoughtful mood, after promising to send him a copy of this book at his own request.

CHAPTER EIGHT

Spiritual Healing

THE PRESENT REVIVAL of interest in healing by the use of spiritual and mental processes alone is certainly a matter for thankfulness. It was not until the third century of our era, when Christianity became a State religion, that the successful practice of healing through the methods used by Jesus fell into disrepute. Church organisations in Britain and America are now beginning to wake up to the fact that they have long neglected their responsibilities in this connection. Resulting from this neglect many organisations outside the orthodox Churches have come into existence during the past half-century. The largest and most successful among these sectarian groups is the Christian Science movement, which now has its own churches and societies throughout the world.

Christian Science healing relies entirely upon the use of prayer combined with mental affirmation. The majority of other organisations established for the purpose of practising healing differ from Christian Science methods in at least one important respect. 'Spiritual healing' as interpreted by such bodies includes not only the use of the forces of the mind, but also the employment of such material aids as the laying on of hands

and co-operation with the medical profession. The use
of psychic methods of diagnosis and the enlistment of
the services of 'spirit doctors' are other ways in which
divergence from Christian Science methods can be
discerned. One result of these developments can be
noted in the increasing interest in non-medical methods
of healing now being shown by doctors themselves.

The immense power of mind over matter, a subject
of ridicule half a century ago, is now becoming a recognised factor in all forms of the healing art. Evidence
is now available to show that certain individuals possess
natural healing powers of a kind that can be transmitted
by the hand and sometimes simply by the presence of
the healer at the patient's bedside.

It seems reasonable to suppose that we all possess
the ability to heal, to a greater or lesser extent. Just as
the clairvoyant faculty can be brought into play through
training and discipline, so is it reasonable to believe
that the capacity to heal mental or bodily diseases by
'spiritual' means can be cultivated. It seems certain that
man is only just beginning to tap the spiritual, mental
and psychic potential with which he is endowed. The
Spirit of Christ is within each one of us, only awaiting
to be aroused and utilised. Why are we so chary in
accepting the vast heritage which is ours?

. . . . .

It is useful to remember the views on healing that
have come down to us from the wisdom of an earlier
age.

> Pythagoras said that the most divine art was that of
> healing. And if the healing art is most divine, it must occupy
> itself with the soul as well as with the body; for no creature
> can be sound so long as the higher part of it is sickly.
> Apollonius of Tyana (d. A.D. 97).

> The physician should know the invisible as well as the
> visible man. . . . There is a great difference between the

power which removes the invisible cause of disease and that which causes merely external effects to disappear.

    Paracelsus 'Paragranum' (A.D. 1493–1541).

If several healers offer themselves—namely, one who heals with the knife, one who heals with herbs, and one who heals with the holy word, it is this one who will best drive away sickness from the body of the faithful.

    The Avestas, Vendidad (*c.* 1000–400 B.C.).

Healing 'Miracles'
(Abdul Baha Abbas)

It has been my good fortune to meet two saintly men whose capacity to heal has seemed to me to be almost as wonderful as that of Jesus Himself.

I have already referred to the Persian seer, Abdul Baha Abbas, a modern-day prophet, whose father, Baha Ullah, founded the Bahai Faith a century ago. This great movement first emerged from the Moslem world and has now become a purifying and regenerating influence far and wide. One of the great purposes inspiring the Bahai Faith is to bring about unity and brotherhood between all religions, with the desire to establish a universal faith that shall embrace all mankind. For a period of over forty years Abdul Baha and his family lived in Turkish prisons, first at Adrianople and later within the walled town of Acca on the Palestine coast. His saintly father died there in 1892 and it was not until the Young Turkish Revolution in 1908 that Abdul Baha secured freedom for his family and himself. They had committed no crime, but their movement was so much feared by the Muslem fanatics in Persia that the Teheran authorities were able to induce the Turkish Government of the notorious Sultan Abdul Hamid to act in this barbaric manner. It was not unusual for devoted followers to make the long journey from Persia to Acca, by mule or on foot, solely for the purpose of receiving their master's blessing, although this could only be obtained through prison bars. Many sick and maimed were brought all this way, taking two or three months on the journey. They would be carried to a spot on the seashore from which a view could be obtained of the barred window on the sea wall of Acca, through which a glimpse of their venerated leader could be obtained.

Although unable to be present on such occasions, I have secured reliable evidence to the effect that many remarkable healings, even of so-called incurable diseases, took place solely as the result of these pilgrimages of faith.

The patients would be carried on to a small rock in the sea which gave the best view of the window behind which Abdul Baha would stand to give his blessing. I have spoken with one of those who was completely cured in this way. He had been bedridden for twenty years and was both dumb and paralysed. His sons had carried him on a stretcher all the way from Tabriz to Acca by road and mule track. He told me that so soon as he saw his beloved master, standing behind these prison bars, with his hands held out in blessing, he felt new life surging throughout his body. (It should be mentioned that there was a distance of over sixty yards between the wall of the prison and the seagirt rock on which the pilgrims were wont to gather.) Within a few minutes of receiving Abdul Baha's blessing, the healing happened. The paralysed man found his voice, stood up and was able to carry his own stretcher back on to the shore. When I met him some years later he told me this story, and one of his sons (who was present when this miracle took place) was able to assure me of its truth in every particular.

After his release in 1908 Abdul Baha went to live on the slopes of Mount Carmel at Haifa, where I often visited him. Later, he was twice my honoured guest in England.

The following incident is worth recording. In the spring of 1910 I went out to Alexandria, where Abdul Baha was staying at the time. I had been entrusted with gifts from his English friends to take to him. I had travelled from Marseilles on a steamer called the *Sphinx* and intended to return overland via Damascus, Smyrna, Constantinople and Vienna. My return ticket and reservations for the round trip were arranged before I left London. On arrival at Alexandria I lost no time in visiting my revered friend and in carrying out the commission with which I had been entrusted. I speak no Persian and my knowledge of Arabic is rudimentary, and so our conversation was carried on through Abdul Baha's grandson, acting as interpreter. At one point the latter was called away, but Abdul Baha continued the conversation and I found myself replying! When the interpreter returned, my ability to do so ceased. To make sure that I had understood correctly, I asked for a translation of what Abdul Baha had been saying in his absence, and this confirmed the fact that I had been able to understand and to reply accurately in a language of which I was completely ignorant. (This curious experience was repeated some years later when visiting Abdul Baha in Paris.)

On returning the next day for another interview, I asked the master to give me his blessing for the journey that lay ahead of me. This he did, adding casually that I should be returning to Marseilles on the following day on the same steamer from which I had so recently disembarked. I then explained to the interpreter that I had made other arrangements and that all my overland bookings had been made. He replied to the effect that if the Master said I had to return to Marseilles now, then that was what would happen.

I went back to my hotel in a state of considerable

annoyance because I saw no good reason for changing my plans. During the night, a very restless one, I found myself in two minds as to what I should do. Next morning, when I went to say goodbye, and much to my own surprise, I told Abdul Baha that in fact I *was* leaving on the *Sphinx* for Marseilles later on that same day. He took this for granted and then requested me to carry out a commission for him on reaching Paris. He said that there I should meet a certain Persian student who was nearly blind, and he gave me £10 in gold to pay his fare to Alexandria. (Travelling was much cheaper in those days!) I was to tell this young man, whose name was Tammadun ul Molk, to lose no time and to present himself to his master as soon as he arrived. I accepted this commission with very bad grace because it seemed a poor reason for upsetting all my previous plans. When I asked for the student's address in Paris I was told that this was unkown, but that a way would be found for bringing me into contact with him.

On reaching Paris I went to the Persian Consulate, only to find that Tammadun ul Molk was unknown to the officials there. I then visited the students' quarter on the left bank of the Seine and spent the whole day there and elsewhere in a task that yielded no results whatever. When one's mind is fearful or depressed, no interior guidance can be expected. This I have found to be true on many occasions throughout my life. In the present instance I gave up the search and set out for the Gare du Nord, where my luggage was already deposited in readiness for the return to England. *En route* I crossed the Seine by the Pont Royale. Happening to look across the bridge to the opposite pavement, I saw, among a crowd of pedestrians, a young man, evidently of Eastern origin, who was using a stick to tap his way along. I dodged through the traffic and accosted him. In reply to my question, he told me he was of Persian origin. I then enquired whether by chance he knew a certain Tammadun ul Molk. In surprise he replied '*C'est moi*', adding that he had only arrived in Paris from Vienna that very morning. In a Vienna clinic three serious operations on his eyes had been undertaken, but the results were negative and he had been told by the surgeon that his sight could not be saved.

I then gave Abdul Baha's message and the £10 for his ticket to Alexandria. To watch the profound joy on his face was more than sufficient reward for all my previous disappointments, including the abandonment of my European tour. Tammadun duly reached Alexandria and visited his master at once. Those present told me later that Abdul Baha poured a few drops of attar of roses into a glass of water. He then gave the youth his blessing whilst anointing his eyes with the water in question. Immediately full sight was restored, and when I met Tammadun some years later he was still enjoying perfect vision.

The further sequel was both significant and instructive. I crossed to England late that night and on reaching my office the next day discovered that I was only just in time to avert a very serious crisis in my affairs. The change in my plans had indeed turned out to be a blessing in disguise.

On many other occasions the prophetic insight of the Bahai leader was made clear to me. As an instance of this, I recall that when visiting him at Haifa, just after the Armistice in November 1918, I spoke of the thankfulness we all must feel that the war 'to end all wars' had been fought and won. Sorrow came into the master's eyes. He laid his hand upon my shoulder and told me that a still greater conflagration lay ahead of humanity. 'It will be largely fought out in the air, on all continents and on the sea. Victory will lie with no one. You, my son, will still be alive to witness this tragedy and to play your part. Beyond and following many tribulations, and through the beneficence of the Supreme One, the most great peace will dawn.'

Abdul Baha left us some years ago and his mortal remains lie buried in a mausoleum on Mount Carmel, specially built for the purpose by devoted followers from many countries.*

Padre Pio

Before proceeding, I should explain that these notes, covering a period of half a century, are written almost entirely from memory. When my London offices were destroyed by enemy action in 1944, my diaries and many other irreplaceable records were lost. No doubt I have slipped up in connection with dates and other historical details. Memory, wonderful faculty that it is, cannot always be brought to the surface at will.

. . . . .

Now let me tell you something about a very saintly healer and visionary who is still alive. Incidentally, how is it that such holy men so rarely seem to emerge in Protestant countries? I refer to a Catholic priest who is known as Padre Pio of Pieltricena in Southern Italy and who comes of peasant stock. From early life he appears to have been gifted with healing and visionary powers. In early manhood he became a Franciscan friar and later entered a famous monastery situated in the Gargano hills not far from Manfredonia. He is now the venerable Abbot there. In 1918, some months before the Armistice, when praying for peace through the night hours, he lost consciousness and was found in the morning lying insensible before the altar of the monastery chapel, bleeding from the stigmata on hands and

* Readers who would care to hear more about the Bahai Faith can obtain such information from the Bahai Publishing Trust, 27 Rutland Gate, London, S.W.7.

feet, which strange phenomenon must have happened during the night.

Some twenty-five years ago, when I was on a visit to Padre Pio, a peasant woman came into the sacristy carrying in her arms a seven-year-old girl of very frail appearance. Her husband followed and he told me that their child had been dumb and paralysed since birth and had never walked or spoken. The child was in an emaciated condition and appeared to be unconscious. Padre Pio caused a rug to be laid on the stone floor of the sacristy and told the mother to lay her child upon it. He then sprinkled water upon the seemingly lifeless form and remained in silent prayer for a long time. Finally, he said in Latin, 'Rise up and walk'. The child stirred, opened her eyes, half smiled, and then sat up. Both parents were on their knees, weeping and praying by turns. Padre Pio then took the child by the hand and very gently raised her to a standing position. Wordless sounds of happiness came from her lips and she was able to stagger a few steps into her mother's arms. Six months later, when visiting the village school at Monte San Angelo, I saw the same child, sane and well, playing happily in the schoolyard.

I could relate many other cases of a similar kind, but what has remained especially in my memory is an incident of another kind with which Padre Pio was connected.

Between the two world wars I was associated with an international group who were engaged in draining and reclaiming the malaria-infested marshlands around the Lago di Lesina near the Adriatic shore. Malaria in its most virulent form had been rampant in these regions since Roman times. We found it impossible to induce the sturdy peasants from the Gargano hills above to come down into this disease-infested valley to work as labourers and artisans. Although poverty-stricken, the high wages offered proved no inducement to these men. Finally I decided to visit Padre Pio and to seek his advice. He showed keen interest in our Bonifica undertaking and told me to let it be known throughout the district that he had blessed the work and all who were engaged upon it. This I did. Within a week over two hundred of the hill folk—men, women and children—had come down from the hills to offer their services. The only accommodation we could provide at the time was a tin shack where meals could be served, and bell tents for sleeping quarters. The deadly mosquito was soon at work, as the necessary netting for protection was in short supply. During a period of over eighteen months not a single case of malaria was reported among them, and our workers finally returned to their hillside and forest homes cheerful and in the best of health.

Padre Pio is now an old man, but still active and deeply venerated. One curious fact about him is that he himself has suffered from poor health since youth, to which is added the grievous and continuous pains resulting from the wounds of the stigmata which have never healed. I have never met a more saintly man or one more imbued with healing power and prophetic vision, but how strange it is that he has evidently made no effort to secure relief from his own bodily ills!

Chapter Nine

The Genie and the Lamp

IF I NOW turn to lighter matters it is because useful lessons can often be learnt from experiences which at the time seem of small account. Recently a friend was anxious to secure a medieval sanctuary lamp for her private chapel. She had searched the shops in London, Manchester, Brighton and elsewhere, but without success. I offered to try to help, but without holding out much hope. Some days later, when travelling into Brighton by bus to do some market shopping, my thoughts turned to the problem of the lamp. Unexpectedly, as is usually the case in such instances, I became aware of the presence near me of a little visitor whom I have since learnt to look upon as 'my little genie'. He was a puckish-looking sprite dressed in green but with a face that showed both humour and intelligence. You will have noted my use of the word 'aware'. Clairvoyant vision does not operate through the eyes, in fact better results often follow when the eyes are closed. To say that one 'sees' beings or objects that are invisible to normal vision is consequently misleading. The mind possesses a vision of its own, one that is independent both of the brain and of physical eyesight. 'Speech' is of course 'silent' except on rare occasions.

These facts should be remembered and the use of such words as 'ask' or 'talk' should not be taken in a literal or three-dimensional sense. The following 'conversation' then took place:

My little genie: What's troubling you?
W. T. P.: I have been asked to find an ancient sanctuary lamp and I don't know where to look for it.
M. L. G.: Fancy worrying about that!
W. T. P.: But I *do*.
M. L. G.: I daresay I can help you. In fact there *is* such a lamp in the place where you are going.
W. T. P.: I don't think so, because all the likely shops there have already been searched without result.
M. L. G.: Don't you believe what I say?
W. T. P.: I might, if you would give me the address where such a lamp can be found.
M. L. G. (*evidently a little touchy*): Very well, if you don't believe me, goodbye. (*And off he went.*)

Just before the journey ended, my little visitor reappeared and seemed to have recovered his good humour.

M. L. G.: I hope you are now sorry for your lack of faith. You don't deserve it, but if you will go into the first shop you see when you leave the bus, you will find what you are looking for.

Then off he went again, dancing away beyond the horizon of my vision. Following the suggestion, but without much hope, I walked into the first shop I saw, which happened to be a modern jeweller's. The assistant who answered my enquiry said no such object could be found anywhere in Brighton, and dismissed me. As I was leaving, the proprietor of the shop came forward and enquired whether he could be of any service. I repeated my enquiry. 'Why, yes,' he replied. 'I do happen to have such a lamp in my cellar, but until now I had quite forgotten all about it.'

After a long search the lamp was duly found and it turned out to be exactly what was required, being a fine specimen of fourteenth-century Italian origin. It has now been cleaned and repaired, and remains lighted night and day before the altar in the private chapel at Adlington in Cheshire.

On other occasions since, my little genie has proved his usefulness. I cannot call him up at will, much to my annoyance. His visits are rare, always unexpected and (so far) only when I am in Brighton or its environs, and nowhere else.

The Genie and the Little Horse

About a year later I was again in Brighton. As I left the Queen's Hotel on the front, my little man came dancing towards me, evidently in high glee.

'Go into the Lanes and buy the little horse,' said he.
W. T. P.: What little horse?
M. L. G.: Never mind, do as you are told or I shall be very angry!

Meekly I turned up into those ancient and narrow alleys called the Lanes and famous for their curio and antique bazaars. I hunted through every shop but found no trace of a horse or any other animal. I then visited the post office near by, posted some letters and bought stamps. On coming out I was met by my little man, who appeared to be almost speechless with fury. 'Go back and do as I told you and I will sharpen your eyesight.' Back I went and, after a further search, finally glimpsed through a grimy window on a back shelf what might have been a small carved animal of some kind. I went in and asked to be shown the object in question. It turned out to be a magnificently carved small Tibetan pony, fashioned out of a lovely piece of mahogany. On asking the price I found that I had insufficient money on me to pay for it. Also, the price was more than I expected.

I went home and told my wife about the incident. Being used to my peculiar ways, she showed no surprise, but urged me to go back to Brighton as soon as possible and not to return without the little horse. A few days later I followed this advice and was fortunate to be just in time. A London dealer, already in the shop, was showing an inconvenient interest in the object which I had come to buy. I succeeded in making the purchase and asked for the name and address of the craftsman who had created this fine piece of carving. He turned out to be a young seafarer who carved as a spare-time hobby and who had never received any training. Subsequently I was able to secure for him regular and interesting employment and so to give him the opportunity to pursue his craft under favourable conditions. The little horse has now been in my possession for several years and I have refused tempting offers for it. Up to now, and so far as I am aware, there seems no particular reason why it should belong to me rather than to a museum or to another collector. My little genie disdains to give me any reason for his insistence in this respect, but perhaps a sequel lies ahead.

The time has come, I think, for me to advise readers not to take the stories related in this chapter too seriously. What may seem reality to me may prove mere fantasy to someone else who had not met with similar experiences. The border-line between what we call imagination and what seems to be reality is hard to define. Perhaps it does not exist? Who can prove that dream life is not nearer reality than the activities of the day?

The dividing line between reality and imagination may be a narrow one. There are, of course, two kinds of imagination: one consists in the vagaries and frivolities of the brain, when it is released temporarily from the control of the mind and of the will. In my view such fantasies are not the product of the creative imagination. True imagination is surely of a different order altogether. It is a gift bestowed upon us by our Creator and should be cherished and treated with respect. As has been said before, all great art—music, sculpture, painting, literature—is the product of divine imagining, a creative capacity with which we have been endowed by God. Every form of life must have originated as images in the Mind of the Creator. When the WORD was spoken, these children of God's Mind were imaged forth into manifestation and, as a result, we live and move and have our being, and cannot be deprived of any of these three. This is my profound belief. I do not voice my convictions in this respect for the purpose of giving any particular importance to the experiences which I am sharing with you now. Each should form his own judgment and, as has been said earlier, I have no desire to convince anyone of the 'truth' of what I write, and am certainly no propagandist in this respect.

Why should we strive to convince each other of anything at all? Truth and reality are not external objects that can be handed round upon a plate. They are the private and interior possession of each one of us, not to be sought for outwardly, but from within. The consciousness of the individual man is capable of infinite extension. It can reach up into the highest heaven or range down into the lowest hell. Its possession should be regarded with the deepest reverence. To assert that man's mind is cosmic in its infinity and in its universality may sound meaningless to you and to me at present. What of it? We have eternity in which to solve the mystery of Creation. There need be no unseemly hurry. We are not the slaves of time and, if we seem to be, then we should begin to awaken now and claim the heritage which is ours through the Love and the Will of God. We can roam the wide world in urgent search for the Holy Grail of Wisdom, and in vain. Sooner or later, this search will end successfully within the self, where in fact it resides already.

In my view, one of the most profound truths ever uttered was voiced by Clement of Alexandria some eighteen centuries ago. It sums up in a single sentence the purpose of human evolution. 'The Word of God became man in order that thou also mayest learn from man how man becomes God.' Or, in another rendering: 'How man becomes God's likeness.'

The Genie and the Storm

On a later occasion I was walking along the Brighton promenade when a violent thunderstorm overtook me and I was soon drenched to the skin. As I turned to run for shelter my little friend appeared and pointed towards a seat fully exposed to wind and rain, where could be seen two figures crouching under a ragged macintosh.

M. L. G.: Go along and stop them.
W. T. P.: Stop them from what?
M. L. G.: Do as I say or I shall be furious with you.

Docilely I approached the seat, sat down upon it and after a while ventured to address the wretched pair. They turned out to be a young West Indian fellow and his girl. They were down on their luck, had nowhere to go and, to make matters worse, the girl said she had just received news of her mother's death at home. They said they had come down from London on foot, with the intention of drowning themselves.

W. T. P. to M. L. G.: What can I do?
M. L. G.: Tell them that the sun will be shining again in a few minutes and that they must cheer up.

Now, if meant literally, this was absurd. The time was near sunset, the downpour continued, there was no wind, and black clouds filled the sky. Thinking M. L. G.'s remark was made for some special purpose and intended to be metaphorical, I told the desperate couple what he had said, but without disclosing who had said it! Then I got up, shook hands, and went my way. Within a few minutes a breeze sprang up from the sea, the clouds parted to the westward and rays from the setting sun lit up the scene. Never before have I witnessed such a dramatic and sudden change in weather conditions. I turned round and hurried back, filled with natural curiosity. There they were standing by the sea rail, bathed in sunlight, and laughing like children. Then they turned and, arm in arm, crossed the drenched road and made their way down a side street, evidently in the best of spirits.

W. T. P.: What will become of them?
M. L. G.: No business of yours. Nothing to worry about. Go home and get into dry clothes.

This I did, still amazed at having been the witness of what was for me an unprecedented incident so strangely linked with a remarkable freak of the weather.

Long life to my little genie and may he never desert me!

CHAPTER TEN

Conscience—A Hound from Heaven

MANY OF THOSE who write books of memoirs or reminiscences sprinkle the contents with the names and exploits of famous or notorious personalities whom the author has met. In the present book I have been careful to draw a veil of anonymity over the identities of such celebrities as have come my way. The only exception to this rule, I think, has been in the case of the Persian seer Abdul Baha, no longer with us, and Padre Pio, the Catholic saint, who is still alive. In a way the following of this rule has seemed a pity, because, as a result, a number of interesting and dramatic experiences in which famous and historical characters have taken part cannot be included in these pages.

It is often surprising to find that those frailties which are associated with lesser mortals should be present also in the lives of many who occupy high and influential places in our affairs. Recently a personage of considerable standing came to talk over his problems with me. It appeared that he had been evading his tax liabilities for many years and now lived in perpetual dread that the Revenue authorities would catch up with him at any moment. His life had become a purgatory. When I enquired why he did not decide to make a clean breast of his position, irrespective of the consequences, he replied that this course of action would be impossible. He said that the payment of his tax arrears, plus penalties, would ruin him. It would involve giving up his lovely country house and estate, his cars, his servants and his clubs. He added that such sacrifices would be unfair to his wife and children and would cut short the education of his sons. I asked his reason for coming to see me. It appeared that he had reached a point at which the need for a confidant had become imperative. He felt he could not take his troubles to his vicar or to his medical advisers. I then enquired whether the fears from which he suffered were caused by pangs of conscience or by his dread of being found out. He confessed that conscience did not trouble him, but the dread of being 'shown up', resulting in the ruin of his career, made confession and reparation impossible. His family and personal reputation must be safeguarded at all costs. So far as I know he is continuing to live what must be a hell on earth, a far worse condition in fact than would result from confession and its consequences. Nothing I could say would make him change his mind.

It is curious that those who deny most vehemently that they are troubled by a conscience should be the very people whom conscience never leaves alone! Conscience can be as much a 'Hound of Heaven' as is pursuit and capture by the spirit of the Christ. In the long run neither can be evaded. Fear is an emotion, whether the result of conscience or of other causes, that can bring a man to downfall. It saps the health, undermines the moral faculty and can never solve a single problem. 'That which I greatly feared has come upon me', was Job's lament. Fear attracts more fear, and as a result of the accumulation that follows, no way out of the morass can be discovered. The fog of depression makes it impossible to think or see either clearly or constructively.

Few will own up to a fear of God, and the dread of a hell in the after-life is no longer a serious cause of anxiety for most people. Man fears his fellow men or the dreaded outcome of mundane circumstances beyond his control. He fears poverty, loss of the regard of his loved ones, the onset of old age and ill health. These are the considerations which weigh with him, whereas the 'fear of God' (the only fear that really matters) rarely enters into his calculations. The true significance of the term 'fear of God' is usually unrecognised; in fact, the word 'fear' as commonly understood is surely not the best word to use in this connection? Awe, reverence and the recognition of His omnipotence need not be looked upon as 'fear', and especially so when the significance of the Creator's everlasting love for all Creation begins to dawn.

When overcome by fear, be the cause what it may, the only sure remedy is to take the fear to God in humble prayer, and thus be enabled to receive the comfort and solace that is Divine.

I have spoken elsewhere of the way in which thoughts and feelings externalise themselves in form in those realms into which we pass at 'death'. And that these forms appear to possess a semi-independent life and to become tangible realities to those responsible for their origin. That mind, and its product thought, influence matter is now widely accepted, but that no material form or object can come into being without a thought behind it is not yet fully recognised. Not only is it correct to say that thoughts are things, but it is also true to affirm that no 'thing' can come into existence without a thought (or a combination of thoughts) both behind and within it.

The world of matter, as we know it today, owes its

structure and present condition to the accumulation over the ages of the totality of the effects created by materialistic thought processes which have been in operation for an unknown but immensely long period.

The belief that God created matter is surely a man-made conception of the functions of One Who is of too pure eyes to behold evil and Who is responsible only for the creation of Spirit and all spiritual states of life and being? According to this thesis it is the mind of man which at a certain stage in evolution 'fell' into an illusory 'substance' called matter which cannot owe its seeming and temporary existence to the Mind of the supreme Creator. Be this as it may, it will not be seriously disputed that the form now inhabited by man and the environment and circumstances surrounding this form are the direct outcome of his thoughts and actions over a past of great duration. We are each the sum total of our thinking, and this thinking makes us what we are today.

When one arrives at a point of vision from which what we think and feel becomes immediately apparent before our eyes, then we shall begin to direct and control our thoughts with extreme care, and thereby cease to remain their prisoners and the slaves of our past errors. Should you find this reasoning to be unsound, what alternative thesis, one that appeals to reason, would you put forward in its place? The primary causes behind events in world history, or in individual lives, should not be sought in happenings that have immediately preceded such events. These causes may, and usually do, owe their origin to the remote past, and no doubt it is possible for a seer to trace the ever-lengthening thread right back from the event itself to its origin. In saying this I am aware that one is on debatable ground, largely because the laws of cause and effect are only dimly recognised at present, and still less understood in their full implications.

Also, how few of us realise that we cannot think unto ourselves alone? The visible and invisible impact of what we think and feel flows forth into the common reservoir to which we all have access, and by which we all are influenced. Your and my thinking can help to uplift the racial consciousness as a whole, or it can have the opposite effect. This I believe to be true not only of what we may term our serious mental activities but also of our day-to-day and seemingly trivial thought-life. The time will come when we shall each learn how to cease from thinking our own thoughts and begin to reflect within our minds the living and eternal 'thoughts' sent forth for our service by our Creator. The meaning of that stupendous phrase 'in Him we live and move (and think) and have our being' will then begin to dawn and we shall find ourselves one step nearer to that peace which passeth understanding.

CHAPTER ELEVEN

Some Spiritual Issues Underlying World Problems

Speech given at the Royal Palace of Het Oude Loo, Holland, on 28th January 1955.

YOUR MAJESTY AND FRIENDS.
It is a great privilege for me as an Englishman to be invited to come and speak here today at this international gathering organised under such gracious and inspired auspices. I appreciate it particularly, because a great portion of my life has been spent in issues associated with international rather than national and personal problems.

I feel that by emphasising the universal brotherhood of all mankind, under the Fatherhood of God, and also by emphasising the importance of 'God as the Founder of the Universe and therefore Invincible', you have sounded a keynote which should inspire all who take part in gatherings of this kind. I believe you are lighting here a beacon that may very well shine around the world.

You also refer in the notes you sent to your speakers that propaganda for any particular Church, society or movement is regarded as being outside the confines of your discussions. Here again I feel how wise you are, because far too many people are engaged upon trying to reform each other, believing that they have secured all of the truth for themselves and overlooking the fact, of course, that Truth is both universal and infinite, ever unfolding to human consciousness. Therefore when speaking on such subjects as these, the very deepest humility is essential, if we are to make any progress whatever.

Another reason which gives me such pleasure to be here today is the fact that we in our little island have always regarded the people of the Netherlands with the most intense admiration, for their courage, their spirit, their integrity of character under oppression and under the tragic encroachments of the sea, meeting their national problems with a pluck that finds an answering echo in our land.

My subject today is 'Some spiritual issues underlying world problems', and in order to disarm criticism at the beginning I should like to say that I am no authority on the subject about which I am speaking. I am talking to you simply as a seeker of Truth, and you must not regard what I say as anything beyond my own personal belief and experience.

There is a widespread belief that world problems can be solved by the use of the human intellect unaided. One is almost inclined to think, however, looking back over the centuries of human history, that the 'pride of the human intellect' is, above all else, the cause of the terrible chaos in which we now find ourselves and our modern so-called 'civilisation', the relations between nation and nation, between people and people and even between individuals themselves.

The idea that any problem, whether it be great or small, international, national, or personal to you or to me, can be solved by the exercise of the human mind *unaided*, without recourse to some form of spiritual guidance from the Source of all wisdom, is undoubtedly

—and I am sure you will agree with me here—a fallacy which has led us to what appears to be a dead end in human history.

When we are considering world problems, when we as ordinary men and women are wondering as to the extent to which we as individuals can best serve our generation, it is perhaps a good thing to remember the great mystery that within each one of us, within you and me, within all men and women, the whole universe exists: the sun, the moon, the stars, the hierarchy of heaven, and the creative power of God. When I speak about 'you' and 'me' in this context I am not referring, of course, to the external man: to the brain, to the physical body or to the human intellect. I am referring to the soul and the spirit at the very centre of our being, where the whole universe exists, and where we are contained and sustained, as individual entities, in the consciousness of God. And if that be true, and I think you will agree with me that all the wisdom handed down to us from the past would indicate that it is so, we are in fact the sons and daughters of God. Therefore the first thing that we can do, or should do, if we wish to pull our weight in helping to solve the terrible problems in the world today, is to see that our own houses are in order, and that the problems affecting our own lives are, to the best of our ability, solved by our seeking humbly for guidance and inspiration from on High. After all, in the last analysis, world problems are a reflection, on a major scale, of your problems and of my problems.

As man reaches understanding within himself and is able to reflect the illumination of the Divine spirit (always waiting to pour down upon him), as he does this, he is doing more than he realises to uplift the consciousness of the whole of the human race, and in so doing has taken the best step he can towards playing his part in helping to solve the great problems of the world.

May I say a few words about Truth? As we go about the world we meet those who tell us that they have found the Truth. They say they have found all the Truth there is. You find this reflected in international affairs by the great ideologies by which the world is split, ideologies held so firmly that those who are responsible for expressing them are prepared to fight and to destroy in order to endeavour to bring converts to their particular point of view. It seems almost impossible (and I am speaking now as an internationalist, not as an Englishman, and not even as a European) for our leaders and for the majority of mankind to remember that you cannot kill an 'idea' with a bomb.

The only effect of physical force when you are dealing with the realm of ideas is to strengthen the very ideas which you believe are evil, by your opposition to them. This seems to me such a fundamental truth, so necessary to be learned by us all, that I do implore you who are associated with the work here to remember that the only way in which you can destroy or transmute an idea which is destructive or evil is by putting in its place in your mind and in your life a better idea. All conflicts, all wars, all the great crises that may still lie ahead of us, are crises of *ideas*. If we would play our part it is on that plane, on the plane of prayer, and of seeking spiritual guidance to help us in what we shall say, and do, and be, that progress can be made, and a solution of such problems found.

As we look around us in the world today, it would appear as if the powers of light and darkness, to use a symbolical phrase, are about evenly balanced, I am not referring now to politics, economics, or social affairs. I am referring to the realm of human thought as manifested by the events that are taking place around us. So evenly balanced appear the forces of light and darkness that the very slightest weight on one side or the other could tip the scales in the direction of progress for humanity or of the coming of the dark ages once more. Here again, we have each a vast responsibility. Every man and woman of good will, of the will-to-good, can affect those scales either towards the darkness or towards the light. It is natural to say: 'How can I, as a single individual, have any appreciable effect on the great cosmic forces that appear at the present time to be in such deadly conflict one with another?'

May I come back to what I said earlier in regard to the great truth that the whole universe is *within you*. What you say and do and think and feel affects the whole universe because the universe is within you. It is all there. The Creative power is there, waiting to be rightly used, and if you rightly use it you are doing more than you realise to tip the scales in the right direction.

There are seers in our midst, who, looking up into the hills, can perceive a new wave of cosmic energy gradually approaching human levels. Here, in all humility, may I say that I am not speaking entirely from hearsay, because in times of deep silence and stillness I have been able to watch the gradual approach towards human horizons of the coming of this remarkable, this tremendous new wave of spiritual life and light. There are many who believe that its approach heralds, and is the preparer of the way for the return of the Christ towards earthly levels. In any case in your own individual deep awareness you will gradually begin, I am sure, to feel and to sense the coming of a new wave of power into human consciousness, available for us as individuals, as communities, as nations, to use for human betterment.

We must remember that as man has a large measure of freewill this cosmic energy can be used on the left path or on the right path. It is for us to decide, having the privilege of this great new outpouring of power placed at our disposal, as to whether we shall use it for the betterment or for the worsening of human relations and our relations with God Himself.

One can take as an analogy the way in which the human intellect has discovered the means for splitting the atom, thereby upsetting the rhythm of the mineral kingdom. The great nuclear energy that results from this discovery is ours to use, either for the betterment of mankind or for the destruction of the human race. At present the omens are not too good.

And so it is with this great new wave of energy that I am speaking about. It is the privilege of our generation to receive, and to use, this most potent power for good or for ill, something that by God's Grace can become the saviour of the world.

Right back through human history, and probably before that extraordinary event which is known biblically as 'The Fall', man was given dominion over what we contemptuously call the 'lower kingdoms of Nature', the mineral, the vegetable, the animal, the kingdom of the waters and the kingdom of the air. It seems to me, and probably you feel the same about it, that having misused this dominion all down the centuries, before we can expect to see peace and brotherhood established in our human kingdom we must begin to make our peace with life in its other forms on our planet, as expressed by the kingdoms about which I have just been speaking.

The mineral kingdom, for instance. What do we do? We tear the minerals out of the earth, and in a large number of cases we use them for the production of armaments, for blasting and destroying life. In many other ways we have interfered with the normal rhythm of the mineral kingdom. We should now begin to make our peace with those intelligences who are in control of that kingdom and whose friendliness we have lost.

And so it is the case with the vegetable kingdom. Here we are poisoning our soil with artificial fertilisers, thereby creating an increase of diseases among plants, animals and human beings. We are cutting down our forests, wastefully using timber, creating artificial deserts. How can it be said that we are using our dominion over the vegetable kingdom in the way in which it should be used or is intended to be used?

And what about the animal kingdom? Breeding to kill and eat, vivisection and all the cruelties which divide us from the animal kingdom, from our brothers and all life upon this planet? Surely the time has come when we should begin, to the extent which is within our power, to make our peace with the animal kingdom!

Then again, in the kingdoms of the water and of the air we have created conditions through racial wrong thinking all down the centuries, and more recently through atomic explosions, and in many other ways, which have gravely upset the natural rhythm of these kingdoms, thereby causing climatic and other elemental upheavals.

If you go up some 80,000 feet into the atmosphere and you have vision, you will find that all round the planet there is a network of an etheric fabric which is a protective garment for our planet itself. And it can be seen that repeated atomic explosions have created rents in this protective 'envelope' through which inimical currents can enter our sphere, allowing all sorts of discordant, unnecessary and unessential forces from outer space to come into our atmosphere and even into our minds. How can we say that we are doing our duty towards the kingdom of the air or the kingdom of the waters?

In Holland it is the element of water through the encroachment of the sea which has always provided a major problem for the nation. In all humility I am going to suggest the wisdom of an entire change of attitude, nationally and individually, towards this dreaded menace. The winds, the tides, the waters of the sea, the rain, are all gifts from God, and if we have upset the rhythm of the laws governing the activity of these elements then it is not for us to place the blame on any other shoulders but our own. In dealing with your great problem of the encroachment of the sea upon your beloved land, why not change your attitude towards this seeming enemy, realising where the fault lies and blessing your enemy rather than cursing him?

Whenever each one of you is on the sea or is using the rivers, waters and canals of your country, and in other ways, why not make a special point of blessing the waters that they may become friendly and co-operative as you become friendly and co-operative towards them? Each time you drink a glass of water remember to bless it and to ask those intelligences in charge of this element for their friendship and understanding, promising to do all that is possible in return to right the wrong that has been done.

Here it is natural for you to say to me that individual effort of this description can surely have very little tangible influence upon one of the great cosmic forces of Nature, but may I remind you once more of the fact about which I spoke at the beginning of this address, that each one of us as an individual contains the universe within his own self, together with that divine spark which makes it possible for your and my individual efforts to become far more potent for good than is generally realised.

. . . . .

In my travels about the world people are constantly coming to me—why I do not know—and asking me 'What can I do with my life to be of service?' There is a very simple way, I think, in which we can all help, and that is by the right use of the power of expectation; the more we can *look up* and expect with faith the victory of light over darkness, dedicating ourselves to selfless service, the surer and the quicker will be the victory. 'What things soever ye desire (expect) when ye pray, believe that ye receive them, and ye shall have them.' Unfortunately it is the habit of the human mind in its fear and unrest to look down to matter, disease, discord and difficulties, forgetting the realisation of Job that 'what I greatly feared has come upon me'.

May I end on a rather personal note? Many people of various races and nationalities come to me with their personal difficulties, which are largely a reflection, in miniature, of the international or world problems now facing the human race. Recently when in Libya an intelligent and thoughtful Arab, in relating the difficulties by which he was personally surrounded, told me that in his view it was as if the very Devil himself had been unloosed in our midst, sowing discord and seeking whom he might devour.

In times of great stress I myself have been tempted sometimes to feel a deep depression, almost as if the Creator had lost touch with His universe, leaving the human race to its own misguided devices. However, at such times I have been greatly helped through being able to change my attitude towards those seeming evils by which humanity is beset. Is it not possible to believe and understand that even Lucifer himself can become the Creator's instrument for good? It is I am sure true that no man is ever faced with problems that are greater than can be dealt with by the inherent spiritual intelligence which stands on guard at the centre of his very being.

Well may we be tempted to feel at times that what may be termed symbolically our struggle with the Devil, or the Evil One, is beyond our power to handle. Nevertheless, it is surely true that through such struggles we gradually learn how to lift ourselves step by step out of darkness into the light of Heaven.

PART II

Chapter One

The Mystery of Dreams

THE HUMAN BRAIN is a peculiar organ and especially so when it is in action whilst the conscious self and the guiding will of the individual owning it are absent or asleep. No doubt all the bodily organs possess a semi-independent life of their own, but with the exception of the brain these organs appear to function automatically, being concerned solely with the mechanics of the body, of which they form part. The human brain, however, seems to possess a particular entity of its own, capable of acting at times independently of the mind. In spite of the theories of the 'experts' who often seem to hide their doubts behind long words, it is questionable whether we know much more about the brain and its relation to the mind than was the case, say, fifty years ago.

The mystery of man's dream life and especially in relation to the time factor remains unsolved. Experiments have been made by firing a gun close to the ear of a man in deep sleep. He awakes immediately and on many occasions relates details of a lengthy dream just experienced, a dream which culminated when the gun was fired, this sound being a natural and integral part and conclusion of the dream itself. It seems correct to believe that a lengthy dream experience can take place within a split second of our 'time'. Then the brain, when unhampered by mental control, seems to possess a strange humour of its own.

Recently I visited a sale to buy a box of tools. The box was a very good one and in my view was worth quite as much as its contents. My bid for this lot was unsuccessful, but the image of the box remained with me. That night 'I' dreamt about a box that at first seemed to resemble the one I had examined the day before. Suddenly it expanded and took on the form of a coffin. Its lid opened and out trooped a group of interesting pygmies who shut the lid and began to dance upon it. This continued for some time and then a large black cat appeared and the little figures hid in fright behind the coffin. The lid opened of its own accord and the cat peered in. Suddenly the lid closed with a snap, trapping the cat's tail as in a vice. The pygmies formed a ring and danced in glee around the unfortunate animal, the cat meanwhile uttering piercing shrieks. At that moment I was awakened by a boy in the street outside crying his wares, which were the early morning edition of a famous newspaper. Now who, or what, was responsible for conjuring up this farrago? It would be beyond the capacity of my imagination when awake to create such a senseless picture. Was it within the province of my brain, unfettered, to enjoy itself in this peculiar way?

I sent out for a copy of the paper, to discover whether its contents could offer any clue. I could find nothing relevant, apart perhaps from the announcement of the death of a man I once knew who had always been devoted to cats and who had travelled in Central Africa where pygmies are to be found. But what is the point of it all and why should we be subject during sleep to such humiliating experiences?

A clear distinction should, I think, be drawn between dreams of this order and actual incidents on another level of consciousness experienced when we are absent or withdrawn from the body.

On occasion I have found myself standing in the cold, looking down on my sleeping form. Sometimes I have 'seen' what was going on in the brain which was apparently out of my control at the time. The 'dream' it was dreaming would form pictures in colour, usually grotesque and far removed from everyday events. Who or what was operating the camera? I would disdain to be responsible on such occasions, except perhaps when certain dreams lose their nightmare effect and become rational or even prophetic.

Premonitions

Accurate premonitions often seem to manifest at the moment of waking from deep sleep. When fully aroused, however, one is inclined to dismiss their validity, even if previous and similar experiences have shown that one can only dismiss such premonitions at one's risk. In this particular sphere of dream 'fantasy', there is one recurring experience which I have never, and rightly, been able to ignore. The milieu of this dream is always the same and it never happens unless a crisis in my life is imminent, a crisis of which I never receive any previous warning. I see a swift dark river sweeping by me as I stand on the nearer bank. The time is always at night and the stars are more brilliant than they ever appear to normal vision. A gloomy barge emerges, manned by unseen oarsmen and gradually approaches the shore on which I stand. At that moment I am aware that if the barge touches land at the spot where I stand, then the time will have come to forsake my mortal coil. If, however, the barge veers away before reaching the bank, then I know (in my dream state) that it is a warning that a serious crisis in my everyday life is imminent.

Needless to say, this strange and sinister vessel has not hitherto 'touched land', otherwise I should not be writing these words. On four out of five occasions, separated by intervals of from three to nine years, when this dream barge has appeared, approached me and then departed whence it came, within a week of the dream itself the crisis it foretold has duly happened. These crises are always of the first-class variety. A ship torpedoed on which I was travelling. Lying gravely wounded on a bare battlefield in the Palestine hills, a railway accident and a serious illness involving a major operation. On the fifth occasion, however, nothing untoward happened so far as I know. What is the object of such warnings? They do not enable one to evade the approaching crisis or to mitigate its effects. The only value they appear to have is to assure one that, however grave the crisis turns out to be, one knows beforehand that it will be survived, even at long odds, because the barge turned away in the nick of time. Who or what produces and directs such dreams as these? It cannot be the brain unaided. Do they emanate from that mysterious entity sometimes referred to as the higher self, or is a benign and intelligent being outside the self at work on one's behalf?

I have often watched in dreams events that are taking place contemporaneously (as I have found out later) in the outer world, perhaps in one's own vicinity, sometimes thousands of miles away. Now and again I have 'seen' events both tragic and comic affecting people I know, from a day to some months *before* such events actually occurred. Rarely have I been able to intervene usefully, as the result of this foreknowledge. On one occasion I was allowed to do so in a matter of some historical and political importance, but details cannot be related now as the events in question are too recent.

Then again, one dreams of places one has never visited, and of strange people met there. Later, when such dreams are fulfilled, it is amusing to know beforehand exactly what the people one meets in the flesh on these occasions will say and do before they say and do it! There seems nothing tangible to be gained by such dreams as these, so far as one can tell at the time.

An Incident at Karnak in Egypt

Once when in my bodily form I was approaching the ruins of the great Temple of Amen Ra at Karnak I saw a procession of priests, chariots and strangely garbed 'astrologers' wending their way around the temple precincts. I took this spectacle to be part of a pageant, a modern re-creation of ancient ceremonies for the purpose of a film, but no cameras were in sight. On nearing the procession I found that my gaze was focused upon the back of a slave boy, dressed for the occasion in a white and girdled robe. He was leading a camel on which some royal or priestly personage was riding. I accompanied the procession at some twenty paces distant from it, whilst willing the boy to turn round and show me his face. Finally he did so and I found myself looking into my own eyes.

I can assure you, if you have never had a similar experience, that there is nothing stranger in life than to come face to face with yourself. And to know beyond all peradventure that this is so.

A Foreign Legionary Meets Himself

In the French Sahara later, I met a man, a deserter from the Foreign Legion, who was at the point of death. He had been without food or water for what he termed 'a moon and a half'. I never discovered his nationality, as there were no papers on him, but from his accent I think he may have been of Teuton origin. When seemingly beyond speech, he half rose from the hollow in the sand where he had tried to take refuge from the sun, and cried out in broken French (I translate), 'Why, there is myself coming to meet me. How wonderful'. Then he fell back and died and we reported the incident on reaching Bou Saäda the next day.

Such incidents make one wonder whether there can be truth in the theory of twin souls, two parts of one whole, who some day will be united. Yet that 'slave boy' to *me* was not my twin soul, or my long-lost brother; he was *me* and no one else, the whole and not a separated part of me. A reincarnation perhaps?

A Waking Dream Experience

During the night following the Karnak temple incident, which took place in January 1919, I was visited by a memorable waking dream.

In the earlier stage of this experience I found myself reliving the incidents of the previous day, but with an important difference. I was no longer only acting as the eye-witness of a royal procession during which my identity seemed to become merged in that of a slave boy, but I was also aware of myself as an objective observer of both past and present incidents associated with the scene unrolling before me.

This phenomenon illustrates the operation of faculties which deserve the serious consideration of students.

It appears that the mind and its agencies are able to perceive happenings and conditions from more than one angle of vision at the same time. By this I mean that the individual called 'I' can act simultaneously as participant and observer. On such occasions both awareness and vision are able to function on two separate and distinct levels of consciousness enabling one to live through experiences whilst at the same time watching oneself so doing from an outside vantage-point. As a result of this dual form of vision, it is possible to 'see' events that have led up to the moment at which one stands and to appreciate the effects of past causes on current happenings. If we refer to the two faculties I have tried to describe as B and C, then there is still a faculty A to be accounted for. I will try to illustrate what I mean. When sitting in my office dictating letters or engaged in a business discussion involving the full use of faculty A, faculties B and C have unexpectedly begun to operate on their own and independently of faculty A's objective activities. On such occasions there never seems to be any link between the material interests and activities occupying faculty A and those with which B and C are concerned. The latter may be dealing with events and experiences perhaps taking place thousands of miles away and often at a different period of time. Subsequently it has proved possible to set down a detailed account of everything that has been seen or heard as the result of the functioning of all three faculties, in the form of at least two and often three distinct and separate records. By this I mean that the brain appears able to register particulars of the experiences of all three faculties of the mind, even when such experiences are taking place simultaneously.

Then of course there is a fourth and still more wonderful faculty involved, which we will call D, namely that of memory! If the reader has been able to follow me so far, then he will find it easier to understand how faculties A, B, C and D can all function at once and from several distinct levels of perception. The above explanation is useful to bear in mind when considering, for instance, the implications of the Karnak experience, to which we shall now return.

In this connection I spoke of a dream that came to me on the night following the meeting with my *alter ego* in the form of an Egyptian slave boy. I should make it clear that the dream in question did not take place during sleep but in the waking state. As faculties B,

C and D were at work in their own departments faculty A was not only registering all that was going on in this respect, but was also able to take note of the clock ticking and of conversations and noises proceeding from the room next to mine in the Luxor hotel, where I was then staying.

As already mentioned, the events of the previous day were repeated in this waking dream, but with the difference that I now became both the participant and the observer of everything going on around me. At the moment when my eyes met those of the slave boy and recognition dawned all four faculties came into play. What follows therefore should be regarded with this fact in mind. The reader should disentangle for himself the diverse operations which go to make up the picture as a whole. Here was I looking at a royal procession. It was headed by the high priests of Amen Ra who had led the way from the altars of sacrifice within the precincts of the temple at Luxor dedicated to this god. I had just witnessed the slaughter of many prisoners and slaves, slain that their blood might propitiate the great god himself. Nothing perpetuated by a Stalin or a Hitler could seem more cruel and terrible. Behind the high priests came lesser priests in robes of white and gold, wearing the ankh upon their foreheads and holding aloft between them the ark boat of the dead. I could see that this boat contained the remains of a royal personage on its way to the river, which it was destined to cross when the sun went down. The cortège would then be rowed across the Nile to the royal wharf and from there the procession would wend its way to Thebes, the traditional burial place for the kings of Upper Egypt between 4000 B.C. and 300 B.C.

The human sacrifices that had been offered up at dawn were for the purpose of averting the wrath of Amen Ra and thereby inducing him to protect one who was of his royal blood on his journey across the Styx. An avenue of sphinxes lined the route from Luxor to the great Theban temple at Karnak, where the principal funeral ceremonies were to take place. I have never seen an edifice raised by human hands which could compare in majesty and size with this vast series of gigantic buildings, as I saw them then.

The hypostyle hall within it with its 134 columns, eighty feet high and over thirty feet in circumference, took my breath away. The funeral procession, with its two thousand priests, servers, acolytes and slaves, having assembled in this hall, seemed to occupy only a fraction of its area, more than fifty thousand square yards in extent. No single building in ancient or modern times can have rivalled it for size and grandeur. When originally constructed the whole of this gigantic edifice was dedicated to the three gods Amen Ra, Mut and Khonsu, a trinity representing the father, the mother and the son.

I stood just inside the inner archway of the main giant portal and for a while watched the strange ceremonies in process at and around the altars which seemed to be placed upon a distant horizon. Being unable to keep my own slave boy in view and tiring of the spectacle, I went my way.... At this point my dream experience appeared to change its dimensions and its form. I next found myself standing below the granite statue of the great Rameses outside his own temple at Thebes across the river. Its height towered into the sky and I could not visualise details of his features from the ground level where I stood.

Next day, for the first time in the flesh, I was to stand beside the fragments of this statue now fallen into a thousand pieces. I was then told by the local guide that this ancient wonder had been hewn from one block of stone weighing over a thousand tons. It is difficult to imagine how a single block of granite of such colossal size could have been hewn out of the quarries at Assuan and conveyed by raft on the long journey down the Nile to its final resting place at Thebes!

But I digress and have in fact done so for a purpose. This is to give readers the chance to pause in order to find out whether they have understood the way in which four faculties of the mind, working both as a team and independently of one another, have each added something of value to the pattern of the narrative?

Perhaps the use of the word 'independent' may prove misleading in one particular. The 'I' who speaks, the individual spirit behind the mind and the senses and usually veiled from view, is in fact the director of the team and is responsible for the cohesion of its separate parts.

The last portion of my waking dream experience has still to be related. It took place at dawn when the rising sun aroused me from my reveries. It was then I remembered that, under circumstances which I cannot now recall, my lot in life had become transformed from that of a slave when maturity was reached. I subsequently became elevated to the position of a priest, one of four, who were jointly responsible for safeguarding the sacred boat and tomb containing the remains of a Pharaoh, whose name escapes me. After the passage of time I saw myself engaged in superintending alterations to the walls of the temple of Queen Hathepsut and I remember how irate I felt at the overpowering brutality shown by the master foreman to the slave workers under the lashes of his whip. I realised then that but for the mercy of the gods, my present lot would have been the same as theirs.

Later still, much later, I found myself living in peaceful retirement in the precincts of a temple built by Thotmes the Second on the Island of the Elephants

THE MYSTERY OF DREAMS

many leagues up-river. It came back to me clearly that I was fortunate indeed to have lived so long. Years earlier I had spent my middle life in and around the Valley of the Kings at Thebes, scheming to bring about the supremacy of Queen Hathepsut, first over her father Thotmes II and then over her brother and husband Thotmes III. Through her influence I had usurped a place of power within the Brotherhood of Priests, several of whom had been 'removed' through the agency of poison provided by the Queen herself. Subsequently I was given a glimpse of the river god who dwells near one of the principal sources of the Nile. I was shown how his influence permeates the waters of the great river over a distance of three thousand miles, a presence that spreads itself across the cultivated land on and near its banks, and finally loses itself beyond the Delta in the oceans of the sea.

· · · · ·

It is evident that the happenings described above must have taken place during the 18th Dynasty, at least fifteen hundred years before Christ. To this day I have been unable to decide whether 'glimpses of the past' of this character can ever serve a useful purpose? Certainly they do not make for tranquillity of mind, and tend to arouse curiosities which may prove disturbing and most unhealthy. I should be interested in hearing if those who have had similar experiences would be inclined to agree with me? It would also be helpful to know whether other students recognise the validity of the thesis I have put forward? I am referring to the four facilities of the mind (A, B, C and D) whose functions I have been trying to elucidate, using the narrative itself for this purpose. If I have not been able to make myself clear I hope the note that follows may prove helpful.

The Soul in Relation to the Spirit and the Mind

So far we have been dealing with the mind and its parts and their relation to the ego and to the brain. It may be wondered why no mention of a man's soul has yet been made. What part does the soul play in the thesis I have tried to outline? The spirit, the mind and the body would seem to form a trinity in themselves, and one naturally would like to know how a man's soul fits into the pattern of his life. Here again we are up against the problem of definition. The ordinary man, or shall I say the average man, because no one can be entirely ordinary, is, I think, inclined to regard the words 'spirit' and 'soul' as synonymous. If this supposition be incorrect, how can the difference between the two be defined? Theologians are usually inclined to refer to the soul of man as something within him which needs to be 'saved'. Rarely is it suggested that it is the spirit and the mind of man that call for salvation. Why the distinction? If I may attempt to apply a definition, I would make the following tentative suggestion, for what it may be worth.

Man's ego, his spiritual selfhood, appears so far as we know to manifest in form. In this context the mind and the body are two of such forms, each functioning within its own territory. Can it be that there is a third and more subtle 'form' available to man? May it not be that the spirit's most ethereal and intimate vehicle of action is his soul, thereby completing a trinity of forms at his disposal, namely soul, mind and body?

On such a suggestion it might perhaps be easier to understand why so much stress is laid on the need for a man to save his soul? It may well be that this garment is so closely associated with the spirit within that its 'salvation' is essential to the ultimate welfare of the spirit itself.

It may be objected that whilst the fate of the physical body is of no account, the fate and the future of the mind is of primary importance to the spirit of the man to whom it belongs. As already said, religious teaching rarely speaks of the need for man's spirit or his mind to be 'saved'. The concentration is upon his soul. There must be some reason for this. If we postulate the theory that the soul contains within itself elements that are both spiritual and mental, then it might be argued that upon the soul's salvation depends the future of the whole man. But what is meant by 'salvation'? Would it be a reasonable assumption to suggest that this process is concerned with the gradual uplifting of the whole man into those spiritual regions and then beyond and above them, where finally the man finds himself at home and once more consciously alive within the Mind of his Creator? The soul may perhaps be regarded as the medium through which the spirit communicates with the mind and vice versa. These metaphysical speculations may perhaps be of little importance, because understanding will come to you and to me, interiorly and naturally, when we are ready to receive it.

Chapter Two

Moussa the Snake-Charmer

Let us now descend from the metaphysical heights and enjoy a little relaxation.

I should like to tell you about my adventures with Sheikh Moussa Mahomed, the famous charmer of snakes. Whether he is still alive I do not know, but as the secrets associated with snake-charming are always handed down from father to son, we can be sure that the Moussa family are still in business. When I first met the Moussa of my time (1919) he was a middle-aged man, bearded, tall and wiry. His eyes were dark and deep-set, and possessed a kind of interior intentness. The red fez he wore was surrounded by a green band to indicate that Moussa had earned his sheikhly status following a pilgrimage to Mecca. The appurtenances of his calling were simple. They consisted of a large sack-lined basket, a pilgrim staff and a flute-like reed. It was soon evident that Moussa took his vocation seriously. Before each operation, which involved the charming and the capture of a snake, a nest of scorpions or poisonous tarantulas, he was in the habit of chanting aloud an invocation to the Prophet Suleiman the Wise and to Mahomed.

We first visited the ruins of the Temple of Memnon,

near Thebes, and stood awhile upon a broken pylon near its entrance. The day was pitilessly hot under a molten sky. Among the ruins there was no sign of life.

Moussa set his basket down upon the sand, tightened the girdle of his robe, stretched out his hands and began to chant a mantra in Arabic, in which the name of Suleiman was constantly repeated. Soon one became aware of a rustling within the crevices of the ruined walls, a rustling both sinister and uncanny in its sound! Then Moussa took his flute and played. There was no action in the 'music' which was keyed to one note, constantly repeated, quiet but wild in tone, and very penetrating.

I asked Moussa what we were to expect and he replied with one word, 'Scorpions'. Almost at once the sand became alive as dozens of these venomous creatures emerged from holes and crevices and began to crawl towards us. Some of them were so enormous that I could hardly believe my eyes. There must have been at least fifty of them, and it was evident that they were crawling towards us, impelled to do so by a kind of hypnotic spell. Some of them appeared to wither and die *en route*. Moussa gathered up the rest and threw them into the basket, where they remained inert. He allowed one of the largest specimens to bite his arm, in demonstration of the fact that all true snake-charmers are immune from poison. The basket was then closed and slung over Moussa's shoulder and we proceeded on our way.

We toiled up into the higher reaches of the royal Valley of the Tombs and it was evident that Moussa was making for a certain spot on the sun-drenched hillside. There, among the boulders which still bore faint inscriptions upon them, we found ourselves before the entrance to a cave. Moussa knelt down and prayed. Then, standing upon a stone, he repeated the ritual that has already been described. Once again I asked him what we were to expect; I did not understand his reply, but gathered later that he was referring to a cobra. Shortly afterwards one of these deadly reptiles could be seen, coiling and uncoiling at the entrance to the cave. Even at a distance it gave the impression of being of enormous girth and length. There seems to be a sinister aura surrounding these reptiles, an aura that can be felt even from a distance of fifty yards away.

Finally this cobra uncoiled anew and began to rear its head and gaze in our direction. Then, infinitely slowly and with devious undulations, it approached the stone on which we stood, reared its head and the upper part of its body and swayed before us as if in submission or in prayer. Moussa stepped off the stone and with his stick made a circle in the sand around our visitor. This was followed by another chant to Suleiman the King. Instantly the cobra subsided on the ground, coiled itself and then appeared to enter into a cataleptic trance. As it was far too big to go into the basket we left it where it was, and moved on. Towards sunset, when we returned that way, it was still there and still immobile within the magic circle on the sand.

By this time Moussa's son Mahmoud had joined us and between them, father and son, the coiled cobra was wrapped in sacking and hauled off to a closed paddock behind Moussa's house some miles away.

At that time, the Egyptian Government was in the habit of paying a fee for every poisonous reptile captured, and no doubt Moussa's well-to-do appearance was evidence of this fact.

By noon we had become exhausted and so we descended into a small oasis not far from the Nile bank. There we found shade and fresh water and made arrangements for a picnic meal. Before lunch, Moussa drew a circle in a patch of sand near by, a circle that was then converted into a narrow trench. Mahmoud stood in its centre whilst Moussa performed his ritual of incantation. Mahmoud then helped his father to open the basket and to tip its contents into the centre of the circle I have just described. It was a sinister experience to watch what followed. Picture a writhing mass of snakes, scorpions, tarantulas and other nameless but venomous creatures as they tried to disentangle themselves from each other and to escape. Whenever one or more of these reptiles reached the circumference of the circle it seemed that some invisible agency prevented passage into freedom. It was as if the shallow trench (no real barrier to progress) was filled with liquid fire.

Whilst Mahmoud sat upon his haunches, cleaning out the basket, Moussa walked round and round the circle, chanting and tapping with his stick. Suddenly the writhing mass within became completely still as if in a state of petrification. Each creature remained in the exact posture that it had occupied the moment before. No sign of life or movement could be observed. Leaving the spot we returned to the oasis, lunched and enjoyed a short siesta.

Before proceeding on our way back into the hills to continue our search, I made a point of returning to the 'magic circle'. Immobility remained complete, and when we came back towards sunset the situation had not changed. Meanwhile Mahmoud had obtained a large sack into which he poured the contents of the basket which contained the captures made during the afternoon's activities. The basket, now being empty, was placed upon the sand and Moussa repeated his previous ritual, but on this occasion he walked round the circle anti-clockwise. Again the stick was tapped and at once life came back, every creature within the circle bursting into violent movement. At a word from his father, Mahmoud walked calmly into the circle and, using his bare hands, gathered his 'flock' together and heaped them into the basket, which Moussa had opened and was holding in his hands. Father and son then left us to convey both the basket and the sack to their home some distance away, and so ended an experience which for me had proved unique.

No true charmer ever kills his captures. If he did so, his powers would cease. By the end of the day I have described, the basket was filled with a writhing mass of scorpions, tarantulas, hooded vipers and hissing snakes. Eventually they would kill each other, but that was no concern of Moussa's. He had broken no law of a kind which he recognised as binding, and on production of his basket and its contents his fee would be assured. When, however, snakes captured in the way described are dead and fees collected, I was told that the charmer performs certain funeral rites before he buries his captures deep in the sands within the sacred valley. Evidently there is a kinship between the charmer and the charmed.

Soon after sunset on the same day, Moussa, with the innate courtesy of an Arab untainted by Western contacts, conducted my companion and myself back across the Nile to the door of our hotel at Luxor. He gave us his blessing in the name of Sulieman the Great and then accepted a fee for his time and services.

In the lounge of the hotel the same evening I met a French doctor who turned out to be an authority on poisons. He told me that in ancient times the profession of snake-charming was regarded with reverence as a holy occupation. He added the interesting information that when the son of a recognised and traditional charmer reached the age of seven, he would be inoculated by his father with a combination of herbal essences and poisons which would immunise the child throughout his life from suffering any serious effects from snake bites which would kill a normal person instantly. One wonders whether the powers so evidently possessed by Moussa and his tribe could not be made available for other uses? For instance, could not the secret knowledge of these strange people be adapted for the cure of malignant disease? I had intended to put this query to Moussa himself before leaving for Assuan the next day, but he was already on his rounds when I sent a messenger to call him. We have not met again.

It should be explained that no casual tourist would be allowed to witness the spectacle I have described. Should he visit Upper Egypt, the dragoman at his hotel would secure on request the service of a snake-charmer. In the hotel courtyard or near at hand, such a visitor would be shown some tricks performed with the use of snakes that had been tamed and whose fangs had been extracted. Nothing more.

In India it may be different, but in Upper Egypt the rules are stringent. Genuine snake magicians belong to a closed corporation among themselves. Probably a secret Order exists which lays down the law. No alien or unbeliever is allowed to witness an exhibition of the kind with which I was allowed to take part. An affinity of sympathy and understanding, which involves a friendly relationship with the Arab mind, must be reached before the door will open. Even then the chances are that nothing very spectacular will follow. This is why I have described my own experiences in so much detail.

CHAPTER THREE

A Personal Note

I THINK THE time has come for me to explain to those readers to whom I am unknown that I am quite an ordinary person. Those who know me fairly well may perhaps wonder at times why I am so interested in the supernatural, but they are usually too polite to show their curiosity. What I find so strange is that the people I meet never seem to have lived anywhere except in the foreground. They appear to have no interesting *background* to their lives, with the result that if I try to share an unusual experience with them, one similar for instance to those that form a portion of this book, they stare at me as if I were in some way abnormal. This makes life difficult at times, because one longs to compare notes with those to whom such or similar incidents are familiar. Probably I have been unlucky in this respect. I sometimes meet those who tell me strange stories of events that have happened to others but rarely can one track down these 'other people'. Usually when one does the stories they tell are not after all 'first hand' but have been related to them by 'other people' still.

Let me add that on rare occasions, and in most unexpected places, I have met men and women remarkable for their spiritual or mental qualities. Healers, seers, prophets, sages, initiates from East and West. All these have come my way and I am the better for the privilege of having met and talked with them. However, I have never contacted knowingly anyone with whom I could exchange views in an intimate way, at the particular level at which I stand myself. This may be my fault. The loneliness of life for one who differs from his fellow men, in ways that are significant and seemingly important, can be very grievous.

There is one problem that has faced me ever since I was a boy. It consists in the fact that I never know for certain whether experiences which are of daily occurrence to me are considered unusual to other people of my time and age. What is no mystery to me seems far too often completely puzzling to those to whom such incidents are related. I cannot find a way for solving this particular problem.

A relative of mine by marriage is a famous mathematician and astronomer. I admire his range of knowledge beyond measure and yet am completely baffled by his mental outlook. Should he by chance read this book, he in turn will, no doubt, be baffled by experiences which to him will seem as mysterious as his are to me. If we are wise we shall not dismiss each other's standpoint out of hand. Rather should we try to look for a place where our minds can meet. Meanwhile he would no doubt be justified in assuring me that whereas his level of thought and action were of benefit to his fellows, the same could not be said for mine. I would hesitate to claim anything in this respect, but it is a pity if such experiences as come my way cannot be made of help to others. This is a matter about which no one can judge for himself, but if the motive is good and one strongly desires to serve those who are in need, opportunities are not too far to seek.

The Uses of Prevision

Often such an occasion presents itself without the seeking. Not long ago a young man came to see me, bringing an introduction from a mutual friend. He was on the point of migrating to South Africa, and at our friend's request I had promised to provide introductions to people I knew in the Union and in Rhodesia. Since leaving the Army this fellow told me he had been working as a bank clerk but that he saw no worth while future there. He said he was leaving his wife and two children in England and that they would join him as soon as he had made good in Africa. After hearing about his capacities and plans, I settled down to dictate letters of introduction for him, which he promised to pick up from my London office later in the day.

Whilst engaged on this task it was borne upon me, beyond any doubt, that what I was doing was a waste of time. It became clear that his present life was to be cut short as the result of an accident and that I was powerless to intervene. What therefore was I to say to him when he returned later that day? Who was responsible for placing an embargo preventing me from offering words of warning? But what warning could I have given? The nature of the danger facing this young man was not revealed and so I went on dictating.

When he called on me later on the same day I was engaged, but my secretary sent in a message to the effect that I was urgently required in the outer office. Apologising for leaving the board meeting I was then attending, I went outside and found that the young man had refused to leave until he had the opportunity to thank me and to say goodbye. He told me he was due to sail in a week's time. Had I anything more I would like to say to him? On the spur of the moment I enquired whether he had made his will and also whether he had insured his life in the interest of his wife and family? He had done neither, but promised that he would do both before sailing, even if he had to borrow money for a solicitor's fee and to cover the first premium on adequate insurance. Then he went his way and I returned to my meeting, sad to think that such a fine young life was so near its earthly end. For the rest of the day an interior refrain kept repeating itself: 'It is not for you to interfere with the destiny of another.' (Years earlier the same refrain had haunted me in connection with an incident in Rome, which is related elsewhere in this book.)

The sequel was as follows. In due course this man boarded the steamer that was to take him to Cape Town, a freighter carrying a few passengers. Having said goodbye to his wife and children, and after they had left for home, he found that he was short of tobacco and cigarettes and returned on shore to buy them. On his way back to the boat, so I was told later, he missed his way among the dock sidings and was run over and killed by a shunting engine. Fortunately his widow was left reasonably provided for from the insurance.

There is no moral to this story. I wish there were. How infinitely preferable to have been allowed to avert a tragedy rather than to be the means of providing for the survivors! What is the value of prevision if it cannot be put to better use than this? The complete answer to this question still evades me.

It is not unusual for people I know to ask me to look forward in their lives and to tell them what I see. On such occasions I am struck dumb. I can 'see' nothing either for them or for myself. With their curiosity unsatisfied, such people are liable to go away with the natural feeling that I am a weaver of strange and unlikely tales—the product of 'imagination'. Who can blame them?

It is my conviction that we are not intended at our present stage of development to peer into the future for the purpose of trying to foresee the character of forthcoming events likely to affect oneself or other people. 'Sufficient for the day' whether it be good or ill, should, I think, remain our watchwords.

I never attempt *consciously* to look into the future, either for myself or for others. When tempted to do so I close my mind to the temptation and go my way. The power of prevision can be dangerous and often brings unhappiness. It is not easy, however, to evade those 'spontaneous' glimpses which may take one unawares. When these concern other people, I have learnt to remain silent. Sometimes, however, foreknowledge of this kind has made it possible to offer useful advice, but without disclosing the reason for doing so.

When a man comes to see me filled with depression at his inability to solve a serious problem, I have occasionally been allowed to 'see' how in the end that problem will be solved. If it be right for me to intervene meanwhile, I realise this right instinctively and proceed to action. If the right is not there and yet I insist on offering advice, the result is usually disastrous. If asked what is meant by the word 'instinct' I am at a loss for a satisfactory definition. I am not referring here to bodily instincts, but to what might be termed that intuitive faculty which is possessed by all to a greater or lesser extent. Whilst it sometimes happens that intuition and reason take opposing views, it is usually unwise to follow intuition blindly without first weighing carefully the pros and cons. It is no more easy to define 'intuition' and to understand what it is than to do the same where 'instinct' is concerned. We are still children in such matters.

'Tell Her to be My Mother'

A lady came to see me to talk over a very intimate problem. She told me that she longed for a child, but her husband had no such desire. My immediate reaction was to explain that no outsider should intervene in such a matter. As I was speaking, a pleasant-looking boy of about six appeared upon the scene and, pointing to my visitor, said, 'Tell her to be my mother', to which I replied, 'Go away and don't try any monkey tricks'. In surprise the lady asked to whom I was speaking. I said I was speaking to her, and, being annoyed, I added rather unkindly that if she could not manage her husband in a better way than she had described, she did not deserve to have one. To soften the blow I said I was sure all would be well, given a little patience and a cessation of resentment. My visitor then left, but not before leaving a five-pound note on the table. So soon as I discovered this I had it returned immediately. Never in my life have I accepted fees for the use of a faculty which, however one may regard it, should be treated with respect. It is not a faculty to be sought (or sold) or to be envied. Its use calls for great care and its availability brings immense responsibilities and the need for discipline and training.

The sequel to the above incident was the arrival of a baby *girl* a year later, happily welcomed by both parents.

The Problem of Evidence

Readers will naturally ask for tangible evidence to prove that these stories are true. How can one supply *outside* evidence to support the truth of *interior* experiences? I have no wish either to be believed or otherwise. Some day we shall no doubt be endowed with wider vision and understanding than is the case at present. Many of the experiences that come my way raise problems which cannot be solved easily. What does it matter? Beyond the duration and perplexities of time Eternity stretches out into the Infinite. What is important, I think, is to avoid snap judgments based on incomplete knowledge and to exercise patience whilst keeping an open mind.

Once before I was visited by another little boy who asked me to arrange for him to be born into a family well known to me. When I told him to mind his own business he replied that it *was* his business and that if he could not arrive in this world through the parents he desired then he would prefer to stay where he was. As a matter of fact he did obtain his desire and some years later I met and recognised him in the flesh. I have no knowledge as to why a discarnate being, awaiting to arrive in this world as a baby, should appear beforehand in the form of a little boy. Why not as a grown man or woman or in some other guise?

The Transience of Existence

A wise man whom I met many years ago in Damascus assured me that our present state of existence is nothing but a transient dream. When I told him about what may be called my 'other-worldly' experiences he replied that these were 'One degree nearer to reality', but still fashioned from the texture of dreams. The search for reality is indeed as elusive as the quest for the Holy Grail, but by the very essence of our make-up the search must go on. Truth in an absolute sense must be like a jewel with a million facets, and no doubt there is a separate doorway into Heaven for each one of us. Perhaps, on the other hand, there may be only one door into those nether regions which we shall probably be fated to visit, if we decide to give up the search for truth? These nether regions are very interesting. Many invaluable lessons can be learnt by visiting them and by talking to those who are compelled to reside there. Such a visit can have more salutary results than the effect of listening to a thousand sermons. I suppose no one is quite free from his own personal hell, here and now, just as no one need be deprived of his own private heaven. Mention of this subject reminds me of a curious incident.

An Experience on the Orient Express

In the spring of 1938 I happened to be travelling to Constantinople on the Orient Express. I had taken a copy of Dante's *Inferno* to read on the journey, and spent some time in speculating on what manner of mind and outlook Dante may have possessed. The train stopped unexpectedly outside a wayside station in Bulgaria. On looking out of the window I was surprised to see a middle-aged man, handsome and well dressed, who was walking along the railway embankment in the snow. He looked down at me, nodded and smiled. The train moved on and very shortly entered a long tunnel. For some reason my carriage remained unlighted. When we came out into daylight I was surprised to find that my friend from the embankment was sitting in the opposite corner of the carriage. Seeing the copy of Dante's masterpiece on the seat beside me, he entered into a most fascinating conversation about the problems of heaven and hell and the enigma of our present state of existence. My companion spoke with an impeccable accent, but evidently he was not English. His clothes and the slant of his mind suggested that he might well be Hungarian. I only wish I had made notes at the time of our very interesting conversation. When the Pullman attendant announced dinner I invited my friendly visitor to dine with me, to which he replied, surprisingly, that he did not eat food. Realising that I was face to face with a mystery, I got up in some confusion and went along the corridor to the dining car. On my return an hour later, my visitor had vanished. The train had not stopped anywhere meanwhile. To this day I am not sure whether I had been talking to a 'visitant' or whether my very charming companion had in fact been clothed in bodily form. There had been nothing to suggest that the latter was not the case.

A few days later I was standing outside the door of my compartment on the platform at Scutari on the Bosphorus. My luggage was already in the train. Once more my friend of the Orient Express appeared; he was standing amongst the crowd some distance away, nodding his head vigorously. Taken aback, I allowed the train to leave without me. Some time later this train was involved in an accident about a hundred and fifty kilometres up the line. Eventually I recovered most of my luggage. Some of it was bloodstained. By then my anger at losing the train and my connections had noticeably subsided. Evidently there are occasions when external influences or intelligences can affect one's life and destiny, but I think such occurrences are very rare. On the other hand, I am satisfied we each possess a benignant guide or guardian of our own, whose services and counsel can be sought and found through prayer when the need arises.

A Case of Intervention

One such instance may be worth recording. When lying gravely wounded in the hills around Jerusalem in December 1917, I prayed for guidance or that my end might come. 'Someone' knelt down beside me and gave me instructions through which my safety was ultimately to be assured. It may be of interest to give the story in some detail, based on notes set down in a Cairo hospital soon after the event in question.

The Saving Presence

It had been a sunny blue day and the scenery was glorious. It was Sunday, December 2nd, 1917, a fortnight before the fall of Jerusalem to Allenby's armies. We were ordered at 8 p.m. to start creeping up the hill of Beit el Fokka a dozen miles north-west of the city and almost overlooking its outskirts. The night was dark; in places the boulders were almost insurmountable. We were able to advance only a few yards at a time. The men (drawn from the Devon Yeomanry, dismounted) were cheery, for they knew little of what lay ahead; only the officers knew, and I for one was satisfied that the enterprise was desperate. The summit of the hill was but half a mile away, though about five hundred feet above us in actual height. We lay down and waited for the rising of the moon. Waiting under such circumstances was not pleasant. The silence was broken only by the cries of jackals.

Suddenly the moon rose across the hills, turning the country into fairyland. We could see for miles, away beyond the orange groves down to the plains and to the sea. It was not long before we were discovered, for there were Turkish snipers behind each ledge and boulder and in the trees. Machine-guns were hidden cleverly at the entrance to caves and ravines; high above were the breastworks on the hill crest, then a bare plateau without cover, and finally the rough walls of an old Roman village on the summit. The first wave of men began to creep forward. The force I commanded was in the second wave, and we followed on, just a few yards every five minutes. . . . In the distance we heard a few stray shots, and then silence. Suddenly chaos was let loose. Shrapnel burst over our heads; machine-gun bullets rained down upon us and how any men in the first wave escaped I cannot tell. The moonlight was in our eyes; we could not fire back accurately. Turkish guns two miles away on another high ledge began to bombard us, and we could not hear our own voices. Men began to fall; some crumpled up without a cry, while others groaned in agony and then lay still. The first wave needed reinforcements, so I took my men up into the front line, running and leaping over and around the rocks, then falling flat to recover breath. . . .

Water was scarce in both armies, and we were fighting for it—fighting for two wells in an old Roman village on the hilltop! Bullets whistled past us, whizzed through the air above. We reached the front line one hundred and fifty feet below the hill-crest, fixed bayonets, and leapt forward on to the crouching Turks. It was a terrible moment. . . . I do not give details because as I jumped over the crest an interior form of guidance began and I was lifted in consciousness above the blood and hell around us. I gathered my men together. The enemy, who had been driven temporarily off the hilltop, swarmed up through the trees under cover of machine-gun fire which raked the ledge on which we lay. We tried vainly to fire over it and down while we flattened ourselves out on the hard rock. Suddenly a score of shrieking Turks jumped on to the ledge, but they never went back. Hundreds were behind them, led by officers dressed in British khaki, shouting in quite good English 'Don't shoot! Don't shoot!' Orders came not to advance, so we lay there, to be picked off one by one, our fire going too high and doing little damage.

We could not dig in, for we lay on the bare rock. Then Mills grenades were sent to us and we pitched them over the ledge more or less blindly. . . . Someone stood by me unseen, a guardian who seemed grave and anxious. I knew my fate would be decided during the next few minutes. I called for reinforcements, and half stood up. There was a Turkish sniper in a fig-tree just visible below but we could not move him. Wails from the enemy came from the woods below, but there was silence on the ridge—those of us who had been struck were beyond pain. . . . I felt a sudden premonition that a decision had been arrived at as to my own fate. The sniper in the fig-tree fired. I fell on my knees, wounded. My sergeant came over to see where I was hit, but fell dead across me, pinning me flat to the ground on that bare bullet-swept ledge. I was bruised and broken, bleeding freely, unable to move. . . .

The sun was rising in all its splendour across the hills of Judah, and there was silence. With pain I raised my head. It was a bitterly cold morning and there was no sign of life around me. What could I do? I longed for another bullet, and just then firing began again. The enemy swept over the hill, bayoneting the wounded, stripping their bodies and throwing them into the wells to contaminate the water. No one who showed signs of life was spared. The protection of the sergeant's body saved me from this final indignity.

Then the unseen presence knelt and told me to lay my head on the ground. I obeyed, and lay still. I heard a whisper in my ear. The substance of the message was that I was needed for some other work later on in life and would not die just then however much I desired to do so. The experience I was passing through would be valuable, especially as a test of faith. The ridge on which I lay could not be held. Had I remained unwounded, my duty would have kept me upon it until I was killed. . . . Later, I heard that no one was left alive there. My 'guide' had come to a decision how to get me away safely. I was to be wounded. I was to lie still for some time longer and make no effort to move whilst my escape was arranged. I must 'obey implicity, faithfully'.

That is all I can remember now, except that the message satisfied me. I just lay still and waited. . . . Probably an hour passed, and then I was 'told' to stir. I raised myself and found that the sergeant's body and rifle had rolled off me and I was free. Beside me there lay a strong hooked stick; I have no idea from whence it came. With its help I drew myself into a position which enabled me to crawl along the ground, though without any clear sense of direction. Later, through the intervention of the same 'guide' already referred to, I was led to a cave where fresh water was available and ultimately to a place of safety.

There is one point about this incident which perhaps is worth recording. Whilst in hospital, the surgeon in whose charge I was told me that the bullet had passed right through my body without touching a vital organ, without severing an artery or breaking any bones, which fact he considered surprising to the point of being miraculous.

· · · · ·

Who decides when intervention of this kind shall be allowed? Who arranges for an intervener to be available when needed? I have written earlier in this book about the mystery of premonitions. Sometimes a premonition of a very simple kind can lead to important consequences.

The story has often been told of a conversation between two young officers in Palestine on the eve of battle. This particular experience took place the night before the incident that I have just related. May I quote the details here?

The following extract is taken from a pamphlet entitled *Round the World at Nine o'clock*.*

The Origin of the Silent Minute

During the fighting in the mountains around Jerusalem early in December 1917, two British officers were discussing the war and its probable aftermath. The conversation took place in a billet on the hillside at the

---

* Published by the Big Ben Council, Parliament Mansions, Westminster, London, S.W.1.

A PERSONAL NOTE

mouth of a cave and on the eve of battle. One of the two, a man of unusual character and vision, realising intuitively that his days on earth were to be shortened, summed up his outlook thus: 'I shall not come through this struggle, like millions of other men in this war; it will be still my destiny to go now. You will survive and live to see a more tragic conflict fought out in every continent and ocean and in the air. When that time comes remember us. We shall long to play our part wherever we may be. Give us the opportunity to do so, for that war for us will be a righteous war. We shall not fight with material weapons then, but we can help you if you will let us. We shall be an unseen but mighty army. Give us the chance to pull our weight. You will still have "time" available as your servant. Lend us a moment of it each day and through your silence give us our opportunity. The power of silence is greater than you know. When those tragic days arrive, do not forget us.'

The above words are quoted from memory and are not literally exact. Next day the speaker was killed. His companion W. T. P. was severely wounded and left temporarily with the enemy, but managed to get back to the British lines with an inescapable sense of miraculous delivery.

It was then that the idea of a daily moment of united prayer and silence was born, now known as the Silent Minute and signalled by the chiming and striking of Big Ben at nine each evening.

. . . . .

Is it not strange to think that a movement destined to become so widespread should owe its birth to the premonitions of a single man as he prepared to take leave of his life on earth?

History has shown that on many occasions the fate of the human race has depended on incidents of a seemingly minor character. I suppose there is a moral to be drawn from this undoubted fact. It is reasonable to believe, for instance, that if Hitler's favourite soothsayer had not predicted victory for Germany, the Second World War might never have occurred. Perhaps it is more reasonable to suppose that the cumulative forces behind any world event, or even behind the happenings in men's lives, are responsible for bringing about the final minor 'incident' through which the powers of Destiny are unleashed?

It may be that when the fate of kings and empires appears to hang upon a single thread, that thread is the instrument through which immense forces operate, and in a way far beyond the range of human vision To think otherwise would make the world picture lying before us at the present time an enigma beyond comprehension to those whose vision is restricted to the immediate present.

CHAPTER FOUR

'Voices'

I WAS SITTING on the deck of a transport in the Eastern Mediterranean. It was at sunset on the evening of November 15th, 1917. The day had been a glorious one, marred only by an attempt made to torpedo our ship during the afternoon. The sun went down in splendid radiance; the sea was still, stars shone up above. There was silence everywhere. I sat alone. Suddenly the night was filled with a tumultuous sound of 'voices'. For a time I could distinguish nothing. I seemed to be surrounded by unseen presences striving, striving, striving to make their voices heard and understood. I could hear voices speaking many tongues: English, French, German, Russian, Italian and many Eastern dialects. The confusion of the sound was great, but, strangely enough, there arose *above* the confusion an Idea. The Idea was clothed in form, but to attempt description would prove impossible. I gazed long upon the Idea that stood before me, striving to understand its purport. The Idea grew out of the babel of voices that surrounded me on every side, welling up out of the sea, and through the air and from the sky. Gradually the voices died away, and then the *form of an Idea* became for an instant more distinct; then disappeared. In that instant I gleaned some inkling of what it stood for, and, taking out my notebook, I jotted down a record of the meaning of those voices. A strange cry from the night, fierce and uncontrolled, sad, but clamourously insistent:

'Our voices *must* be heard. Some day our voices will be heard. No power can hold back from us the chance to say that which awaits our utterance. What is it that we have the need to say? Why should we not remain silent whilst the world groans on in agony? Our message must be delivered, come what may, a message that shall in some degree express the ideas, the ideals of a countless number of us, slain on the battlefields of Europe and elsewhere, slain needlessly, uselessly and as if unendingly. The great ones of the world talk of the Wars that are to follow, as if human conflict would never cease. On this subject we have the right to make our voices heard, voices that cannot be stilled until our message has been given. Because our bodies have been taken from us, snatched away when strength and vigour were at their height, who dare deny to us the right to speak back across the river we have just crossed? Who dare to erect barriers of unbelief, saying we are dead and gone for ever? Because a cruel fate has robbed us of our earthly lives of usefulness, robbed us of our human birthright, hurled us across space into a strange and solemn land, this is no reason why we should not speak that which is in us, pass back our message into those regions where chaos and carnage still mercilessly riot. We are of every race, our message is for every race, we know no barriers of colour, creed or sex. We claim our right to be heard above the din of earthly conflict. Again we say, who dare deny us this? Life itself cannot be taken from us, for God alone can give life and take it away. We have been robbed not of life, but of the form in which we were expressing it. Our opportunities of service and experience have been cut in two. Beyond again will come a day of judgment. Beyond once more will come a day of reparation and repentance. Then will dawn the days of peace. Our bodies lie broken and buried beneath a hundred battlefields, but our souls live on, we have triumphed over death in ways not yet apparent even to ourselves. Listen to what we have to say, for have we not the right to speak our minds? Is it for no great end that we have been murdered wilfully? Who are we who speak to you? By whose authority do we speak? You wish to know? Then you shall hear:

I am a French soldier, I fought in many battles, was wounded thrice, suffered unspeakably, was taken prisoner, died a death of misery—cold, hungry, covered with disease. Shall I tell you of the agony suffered by my wife, my children, my mother? The story is too tragic in its holiness. I dare not speak of it. What has the world gained through the terrors of my life and death? Tell me.

. . . . .

I am a Belgian girl. I died in the market square, naked and alone. Can I never banish from my thought the horrors of my last hours on earth? I was torn from my home, stripped naked and thrown on the ground in the public place. It was evening: I looked up to the quiet stars above and longed for death. Death was so long in coming. I lay upon the pathway of my Calvary all night—and longer still. Can you picture what this means? The enemy soldiers had just come in that first and awful night. They were drunk, they stood in jeering groups around me and used my body for their sensual satisfaction. They brought my mother, my father, my young sisters, and forced them to watch my agony, my shame. Need I say more? Death came at last, at last, and I am here. Some day peace may come to me again, or, better still, oblivion. And I am only one of countless many. Countless many. What has the world gained through the terror of my life and death? Tell me.

. . . . .

I was a Russian peasant, full of lusty youth, of life, of hope. A shell struck me; an arm was torn away. I remained for hours upon the battlefield until I bled to death. I died alone, in mortal agony. I died alone. Nothing can efface the memory. I can speak but little of the thoughts that well within, but tell me this: What has the world or my country gained through me? What has become of me?

. . . . .

I was in the Prussian Guard. I served my fatherland well for nearly three years of war. Why should I not speak? I see my country writhe in agony and still the dance of death goes on and on. I met my death from English gas. For two days I lay outside the parapet slowly suffocating, gasping my life away in froth and blood. I speak for thousands of my countrymen. Our voices blend with those who speak to you across the gulf. War must for ever cease.

. . . . .

You know my voice of old. I can claim your friendship from the days I spent on earth. You know my story well. I was shot at sunset just outside the lines in France. I died quickly. What do details matter? Sufficient that I am still alive. My work here brings me into touch with the maimed and weary ones who die on battlefields. Add my words to those already spoken to you by other soldiers killed in battle. We dare not think we died in vain.

. . . . .

'Who are we to speak to you? Our voices blend, our message is the same, yet, as we have already told you, we belong to every race, we no longer fight among ourselves. We only strive to speak, to give our message, to make our influence felt and understood. To give our individual stories would be to tell unending tragedies of war; to tell of vilest passions, hideous crimes, lusts unending, evils unspeakable, called into being by the trumpets of the conflict. For us, all this is over. We have not returned to speak of what has been, but to speak of what shall be—what must be, if the race is not to be swallowed up for ever in the darkness of unending night. We claim the right to give our message; we command attention. Mark well our words. . . . We dare not rest while wars continue. There can be no blissful heaven for any one of us while the anguish of the battlefields remains. We tell you this. We work that wars shall end for ever. There are millions of us now. We work in bands, in councils, in communities. We are behind the people's cry for peace in every land. We strive in Russia that the people's voice be heard. In every conflict we are there to urge our cause. Think you we have no power? Our power grows and in time will become greater than any power the war lords of the world can raise against us.

'We inspire many who know not of our presence. We stand behind kings. We sit in council halls. We walk at noonday in the market places of the world. We are never absent from the battlefields. We move in and out of the minds of the great ones of the earth, and all, unknowingly, they fear us. We sit beside priests and ministers in their private hours. When they descend from pulpits, having preached of righteous war, we give them war within themselves instead of peace. We dog the footsteps of all who dare to take the name of God in vain. They cry to Him forsooth for victory for this or that material cause. They cry in vain. God is not near such men and will not help them.

'We sit beside our soldier pals in trench and bivouac and hut. They know us not, but all unconsciously they feel our presence and our thoughts. War must for ever cease! Our powers will grow apace. The time will come when we shall bring mortal fear into the hearts of all who dare to stand before our way. We strive, oh, *how* we strive, to make our voices heard above the mortal din. No mundane power can hold us back. We will be heard. We are purposeful, fiercely unrelenting, strong in our demands, united in our strength.

'No man dare tell us we have died in vain. No man dare stand between us and the purpose we are pledged to carry through.

'Our message is to all. Hearken before it be too late. We would avert a chaos beyond words menacing. Listen to our words! A people's peace, a soldiers' peace, a peace such as a child would make—that is the peace that must be made.

'There must needs be renunciation, sacrifice, penitence from all. We see signs, we see blessed signs upon the dim, the very dim, horizon. Meanwhile we cannot rest and would not. Tell the common people of the world, the simple souls, those who suffer silently in trenches or elsewhere, the quiet and steadfast men and women who watch and wait and pray. Tell them that we are with them. We dare not watch, we work. We dare not wait, we act. We cannot pray. We yearn for the day when we can kneel before our God once more and tell Him that the great purpose to which we have bent our very selves has been won—achieved, accomplished. You who fight in war! Soon you will hear the voices of us who fight for peace: who fight across the veil; who fight the long night through.

'One word more. A lesson we find hard to learn, a lesson all must heed. Peace comes to those who are at peace within. Such inner peace is worth a thousand victories on the outer battlefields of life. Be quiet! Listen for that inner voice! The still, small voice—obey it! Never act without its mandate first. Purify the sanctuary within your soul, that the Christ may walk therein. Bar not the gates. The Christ awaits without.

He is calling everywhere. Above the deafening noise of battlefields we hear His Voice. His Message is greater than any we can give. Listen for that still, small voice. Live with it, hearken to it, and all will yet be well. We have spoken. We can say no more. There is nothing more to say!'

· · · · ·

I have recorded above a message that has come down from the First World War. As a footnote I should like to add what follows in the words of a soldier who is still on earth and who is still suffering from the dark agonies of the Second World War.

I met him some years ago whilst on my travels and have since done what lay in my power to help him to forget the past and to face forward into the future with hope and courage. I give his own words, in translation, to the best of my ability. He shall remain anonymous and it matters little on which side he fought because what he has to say transcends the barriers of nation, race or creed. The message of his experience is for us all and its implications can only be dismissed at our peril, whoever we may be.

Here is a summary of what he told me, haltingly and from the depths of great suffering and distress.

In 1939 I was still at school, strong, happy, filled with the joy of living. When the war started I was nearing my eighteenth year, preparing to go on to a university to complete my training to become a lawyer. I came of a well-to-do family and had been brought up in an atmosphere of culture and great comfort. I was an only son and my future looked bright indeed. In those days I felt on the top of the world. Now I am in the abyss, and cannot escape from the black memories of the war years and what they did to me.

I was called up in the autumn of 1939 and drafted almost at once into a unit of a special kind to be trained for service in a branch of the Army equivalent to what has since become known to some as Commandos or Shock troops.

There were about two hundred of us at that time and at that place and our instructors were men of brutality beyond description. I have often wondered since how any nation calling itself Christian could sanction and tolerate what we were called upon to endure and to carry out in the name of 'patriotism'. Our training had but one end in view, namely to teach us the best methods for using our bodies and our hands to murder other men silently and with speed.

We were not allowed to practise with any weapons except the knife, but we were told that the knife was only for self-defence and that our hands alone were to be our main weapon of attack.

Long before I went on active service all light had gone out of my life and all hope for the future. I had become simply a machine for murder, cruelly dominated to a point where freewill and the sense of personality had disappeared.

There were occasions during our training when we were shown how to creep up silently behind sentinels and watch-guards to take them unawares and to extinguish life by throttling. We were even shown examples.

I lived through the whole war as in a nightmare and am only sorry now that I did not finish myself by committing suicide. Our activities ranged through several theatres of conflict in Europe and in Africa and our work was carried out to a large extent behind the enemy lines. In the end I was one of five out of our original number who remained unscathed and still alive.

Yes, I have murdered men, often in cold blood and without the 'solace' resulting from the heat of battle. My hands can never be clean again. Many times all that was left of my better self stood up before me and cried 'Don't do it—don't do it'. To my unutterable shame and on each such occasion I did it, I did it. When at long last I was discharged and returned home I felt an outcast, quite incapable of picking up the threads of my existence as a man. I have become a stranger to my own kin and am now a wanderer and alone.

The girl I loved so dearly has never ceased to wait for me, but I dare not marry, nor have I the right to bring children into this world or to hear myself called 'Father'.

Help me if you can, lest I lose what measure of sanity still remains, help me to forgive and to forget and to pray ceaselessly for those whom I have killed in the cause of 'Christian patriotism' (For God and country).

I have only one desire left, that my story and my example may stir the conscience of mankind so that all who prepare for further wars and who train future generations in the art of murder may be driven for ever from power in the councils of the people and expelled from the governments of all nations.

CHAPTER FIVE

The Problem of Survival

SINCE THE TURN of the century, and especially so following the 1914–1918 upheaval, interest in questions involving human survival and the conditions to be expected after 'death' has quickened. Before the Reformation, Christians rarely queried the possibility that life for the individual might end with the dissolution of the body. It is difficult to understand why anxiety on this subject should have become so widespread in recent times. Prayers for those who are no longer with us are rarely heard in Protestant churches. Prayers for the sick are still a feature of the services in many churches. One often hears the remark: 'Do you know that Mr. X is being prayed for in church? He must be dying.' When death does occur, the prayers usually cease. Sometimes when reference is made to the Christian Fathers, or to the saints, it is suggested by inference that they may still be alive 'behind the veil', but our religious leaders rarely seem able to give clear guidance about the after life of a kind that will bring solace and understanding to the bereaved. How strange it is that Communists and those who believe with them that our personal lives have no future before them seem in no way perturbed by this terrifying thought.

THE PROBLEM OF SURVIVAL

On the other hand, the fear of 'death' is very prevalent among many who profess and call themselves Christians. This subject interests me very much because clergy and ministers who have sought my views often find it difficult to give satisfying and illuminating guidance to those who seek their help. It may be that one result of this unhappy state of affairs is the fact that the modern Spiritualist movement has established its own church organisations and has attracted numbers of Christian people away from the orthodox church communities. I have found that many clergy are as anxious for enlightenment on this important subject as those whom they serve as spiritual advisers.

It is my hope that the relation of a few of my own 'other-worldly' experiences may prove of some service in widening the horizons of those who are perplexed and who find that the teaching of the Churches as a whole does not satisfy their needs or alleviate their fears of what the future may hold in store for them. The majority of people I meet do not credit the possibility that anyone can leave his earthly body until 'death' brings this release. A minority has begun to realise that during sleep, and sometimes on other occasions, a man can function consciously on a different level of being whilst his body remains quiescent. It is not easy for me to understand why this possibility is frowned upon by many religious leaders and why the very idea is regarded as non-Christian and therefore repugnant. In such a vital matter one can only speak from personal experience.

To say that I am as much at home when 'absent from my body' as I am when imprisoned in the flesh may now have become apparent to readers of this book. I do not deny the fact that discipline and long training are essential before the novice should attempt to leave his body during waking hours. During sleep, however, when the brain and body are relaxed, supernatural experiences are far more common than is generally supposed. It is here that the faculty of memory seems to be at fault. The brain, for reasons of its own, hates to recognise the possibility that the mind can operate *consciously* without using the brain as its instrument for the purpose. This may well be one of the reasons why the memory of such experiences is so often cut off at the moment of waking from sleep. The brain strives to dominate the mental and physical processes of man to the exclusion of any other agency. We have come to regard it as our master and not as our servant. I have tried to deal with this problem in a booklet entitled *The Mind Set Free*.* I believe that most people still consider that the brain is the sole medium through which thought can be expressed. How can they explain the fact that enlightenment often comes when the brain is still and that it is only after such enlightenment has been realised interiorly that the brain is called upon to transmit the fruits of such enlightenment to the external senses?

To return to the central question, one that is constantly being put to me in the following terms: 'What tangible evidence or scientific proof exists for believing that I as an individual continue to exist when my body is no more?' 'How can I be sure that the survival of my human personality, if indeed it be true that it does survive, is not temporary and that there is no danger of my being absorbed into the great unknown, or extinguished altogether?'

In view of the wealth of religious and psychic literature now available, it is surprising that such questions should continue to be posed seriously and with such evident anxiety even by those who call themselves Christians. Christ made it abundantly clear that the Creator's greatest gift to man was the gift of eternal life, but His words seem to carry little weight in the

* J. M. Watkins, London.

THE PROBLEM OF SURVIVAL

modern world. If we are all destined to be absorbed in a common vacuum, then the Divine promise of eternal life becomes a mockery.

It is difficult for me to treat these doubts about human survival seriously. The first step in the direction of *solving* this problem is, to my way of thinking, the need to make a drastic change in our conception of 'Time'. Time as we know it is a man-made system for measuring the duration of material events. Its usefulness ceases when we pass from three-dimensional conditions into wider spheres of consciousness. The mind and spirit of man need not be confined within Time's prison house, even while we are still on earth. It is here again that the brain tries to dominate the activities of man. Time, as we know it, is unable to extend its tyranny beyond the world of matter. So long as we believe that it can do so the meaning of eternity will elude us.

Time and Timelessness

When one stands erect and free from mortal trammels time at once loses its power of domination and the brain can no longer act as master. When such freedom has been achieved, the meaning and reality of eternal life becomes apparent. I cannot expect you to believe this until you yourself have experienced personally the freedom of which I speak. If this means waiting until you 'die', well, no great matter. Whether we recognise it or not, we are everlastingly alive in the eternal NOW. As this truth dawns it will be found that most of our problems have ceased to exist.

Meanwhile it should be realised that the laws of physics cannot be applied to metaphysics or to the realms of mind and spirit.

No terrestrial yardstick is capable of measuring the measureless.

For this reason the value of the experiences related

in this book cannot be assessed scientifically. The evidence they contain must be looked for within the experiences themselves. External confirmation lies beyond the range of possibility. As has been said before, this is why those who demand 'scientific proof' of survival are doomed to disappointment.

CHAPTER SIX

Seven Facets of the Mind

I HAVE BEEN driven to the conclusion that the human brain is incapable of registering clearly any idea which cannot be expressed in writing or in speech. We are now entering a region of ideas for which no words have yet been invented. This is why the brain can be of little service in this context.

I am prepared to be challenged as to the truth of this statement—indeed, I should be interested to hear what alternative and satisfactory theory can be put forward in its place.

If, however, you accept my thesis, then it will be realised that what follows can only be expected to reveal a faint glimmer of significance to those readers who rely upon the brain as the sole source of enlightenment.

I have spoken earlier about four distinct faculties possessed by the mind of individual man, viewed from the standpoint of his present existence. For purposes of convenience these faculties have been labelled with the first four letters of the alphabet. Faculty A could be described as belonging to that portion of the mind which functions through the brain and *in no other way*.

This faculty or, if you prefer the term, this facet of the mind is concerned exclusively with events and activities taking place within the confines of the world of matter.

It will be objected that no part of the mind can be confined solely within the closed circuit of three-dimensional conditions. This is no doubt correct, nevertheless I insist that my faculty A cannot manifest or operate without the co-operation of the brain. The daily actions and affairs of most people are dominated by this faculty.

It is probable that many of us are unaware of the existence of any other facet of mind or consciousness than the one described above. So much for A.

If it has proved difficult to define A, how impossible it is to find words that could give an accurate description of B and C! We can, however, start by saying that neither of these two is dependent upon the brain for the fulfilment of its functions. These functions are carried on in regions of four dimensions where the barriers of time and space are non-existent. It is only our faculty A that cannot transcend these barriers, beyond which it would appear to remain completely dormant.

I have already mentioned the way in which the ego can employ mental processes, involving two levels of vision simultaneously, the level of a participant and that of an outside observer. For convenience sake I use the letter B to represent the activities of the participant, and the letter C to represent those of the observer or the watcher. Already we are in deep water, being in a region where the use of words may obscure the issues rather than help to clarify them. However, let us struggle on.

Perhaps an illustration of how B and C can work together may prove helpful. In a book called *The Upper Room** I have described a visit to a house in Jerusalem

---

* *The Upper Room*. Published by the Chalice Well Trust, Glastonbury, 5s. 6d. post free. Also obtainable from Neville Spearman Ltd.—*Editor*.

where the Last Supper was held. This visit resulted from a revival of memory enabling this glimpse from the past to be recollected and re-lived. Faculty A was not employed because my body and my brain were not present on that occasion, but 'I' was there. Through the use of faculty B I was able to visit the house in question and to note in detail, amongst much else, the furnishings of the Table and the Upper Room itself. I could exchange views with my companion and with the good man of the house, and I could also record such views. To do so, it was necessary to call faculty D (memory) into action. Meanwhile, however, my faculty C was able to act as an observer of the scene, not only so, but to extend the range of my and its awareness to places outside the house, to visit a donkey in its shed, to note that the household well in the back courtyard was nearly dry and so on. I presume to think, subject to correction, that without the agency of D (memory) neither B nor C could operate in any manner comprehensible to one's reasoning powers. Perhaps I should add that the use of reason and intuition, to a greater or lesser extent, can and usually is employed in connection with all four faculties, in accordance with the individual needs of each of them.

On re-reading what has just been written, I doubt whether the reader will have any conception of what I am trying to explain! You have been warned already that no words have yet been invented which can give a clear picture of the meaning and activities of B and C. But deeper waters still flow ahead. It is believed, and with some truth I feel, that the mind available to each one of us contains seven separate faculties in all. If we use the simile of a six-pointed star, then it can be said that three points of this star radiate upward, and three radiate in a downward direction. These three downward radiations correspond to our A, B, and C.

D (memory) operates as the essential intermediary between the upper and lower sections of the star.

For convenience, let us refer to the three 'upward' radiations as E, F and G. These three are sometimes referred to as the servants of the spirit of the mind, whereas A, B and C can be regarded as the servants of the body of the mind, with faculty D as the link between the conscious and the (so called) unconscious facets of the mind.

E, F and G function in regions so far above our present ken that, for all practical purposes, even their existence is unknown to us at the point of evolution at which we now stand. This is a dangerous generalisation, but let it pass. Now, in spite of what has just been said, it is, I believe, correct to assert that as the mind as a whole is a sum total of its parts, there can be no rigid barrier between these parts, which no doubt are capable of influencing one another and co-operating when the need arises. If this sounds nonsense it is only because I cannot find words that will embody clearly the ideas I am trying to express. For the same reason, it would be useless to attempt to describe the attributes of faculties E, F and G or to give you an idea of what their functions are in relation to A, B and C.

All that can be usefully said is that these three higher faculties of the mind are not concerned with the activities of man within the limitations of time, space and form (matter). Beyond the immeasurable fullness of time, eternity extends into the infinite, a conception that is incomprehensible to us at present. The experience of the mystic may touch the fringe of infinitude through the use of the three higher mental faculties (E, F and G) which I have ventured to describe as being the servants of the spirit of the mind.

I have made no attempt to include in this book experiences that have come my way at this high cosmic level. No useful purpose is served in my view by trying to describe the indescribable. In this field, however, I can warmly recommend the writings of Dr. Raynor C. Johnson, whose book, *Watcher on the Hills** contains a valuable summary of the mystical experiences of men and women in modern times with interesting references to the teaching of the great mystics of the past.

· · · · ·

To return to our central theme perhaps an analogy can be drawn in one respect between the working of the bodily organs and the activities associated with the various segments of the mind. Such an analogy should not be stretched too far; in fact I am by no means sure that it should be used at all. In a certain sense each organ of the body is a unit within itself. This unit possesses sufficient instinctive intelligence to perform its functions and to respond to messages which it may receive from the brain through the avenues of the nerves and blood. The poise and health of the whole body depends upon harmonious co-ordination and co-operation between all its organs. For the purpose of the picture we must postulate that the human 'I' that is in control is centred within the brain. In a similar manner, each of the seven segments of the mind possesses an intelligent capacity of its own. These seven parts can be regarded as the organs of the mind and perform their separate duties in a way that is similar to the organs of the body. The 'I' that is in control dwells at the centre of his universe just as the bodily 'I' is situated within the brain. This 'I' is the spirit of the man. God-created, it is eternal in being and indestructible in essence. This 'I' clothes itself in various forms and conditions, which change from time to time in accordance with the needs of the occasion. During its career (if one can use such an inadequate expression) in the so-called worlds of phenomena, it may circulate in and through seven distinct spheres of manifestation

* Hodder & Stoughton, London.

and 'life'. Ultimately and at a point far beyond human calculation, this 'I' returns to its Creator, perfect, and enriched by experiences that have occupied a 'period' of quite immeasurable 'duration'. That is the picture I put before my readers. It is for them to decide whether it contains for them an element of truth.

I shall be asked what useful purpose can be served by putting forward metaphysical speculations of this kind? I have two reasons for doing so. Firstly, to stimulate thinking beyond the present range of our horizons. Good may result therefrom. Secondly, to throw out clues which, if they can be perceived, may help the reader to understand more clearly the conditions through which the experiences related elsewhere in this book could happen and the mental agencies employed for recording and explaining them.

When the brain and body die, faculty A becomes quiescent in the same way that, for the majority of people, B and C appear to remain inactive during life on earth. Faculty D (memory) acts as a permanent link between A, B and C, although after the death of the body its methods of operation change in order to conform with the conditions resulting from the transfer of activity from A to B and C. Without the gift of memory, life on any plane of being would have little meaning. It is the function of memory to guide and ensure our progress and our growth as we pass forward and onward from one state of consciousness to the next, in a sequence both orderly and divinely planned. It is for this reason that, as I have already said, your life and mine would possess no meaning if memory were non-existent. This faculty acts as the medium through which in due course all the other six faculties mentioned will become fully integrated as man regains his freedom and progresses towards perfection. 'God is good and man is created in His image and likeness.' In the eternal sense this statement of a fundamental truth must surely be accepted, as applying to the spirit of man and not to the forms he inhabits temporarily, either on earth or in any other world of phenomena.

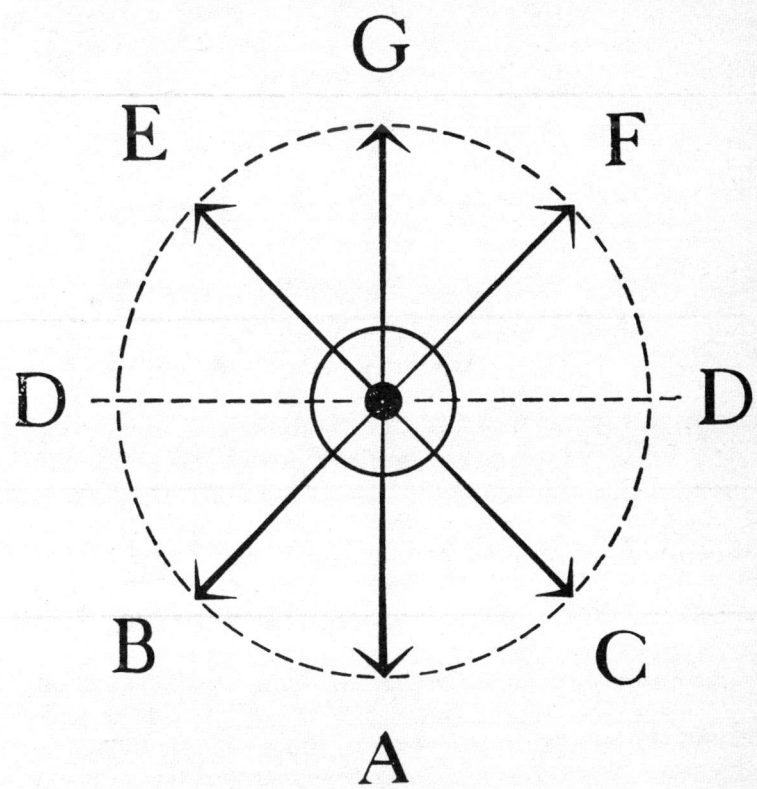

The lower facets of the mind.
    A. Mind action through the brain.
    B. Mind as unseen Participant.
    C. Mind as unseen Observer.

    D. Memory as integrating link.

The higher facets of the mind.
    E. Mind on the Ray of Seership.
    F. Mind as healer and Teacher
    G. Mind in Communion with its Source (God).
    ⊙ The Ego or spirit of man clothed in the garment of his soul.

CHAPTER SEVEN

The Lure of Ancient Egypt

'For the King's House in the Desert'
The Pyramids and the Sphinx Revisited
(Written in 1917)

I HAVE JUST enjoyed a most interesting experience. I have revisited the Ghizeh pyramids and the ruined temples surrounding them, piloted by Malaby Firth, the well-known Egyptologist. He was in charge of the excavations undertaken in 1906 by the Harvard University authorities which resulted in the discovery of the ruins of the Upper Temple of the third pyramid.

We first explored the Great Pyramid of the Pharaoh Cheops, the largest and the oldest of the three, completed about 2900 B.C. This is said to be the most imposing stone edifice in the world that is still extant. At the very centre of this pyramid, in the King's Chamber, we examined the stone sarcophagus that once contained the mummy of Cheops, known in ancient times as the Pharaoh Khufu. That this vast building which has exercised such an immense influence upon the imagination of the race for nearly five thousand years should have been built solely to become a tomb seems most unlikely. Its orientation and measurements suggest that it was also erected for the purpose of becoming an important astrological landmark, one that was intended to give prophetic guidance to seers and occultists throughout the world.

There it stands, in gigantic symmetry towering up out of the desert sands towards the sky. Its proportions are so perfect that one only becomes gradually aware of its immense height and girth. There is something magnetic about this monument, a strange influence pours forth from it. Students of the mysteries tried to explain the symbolic significance of the Great Pyramid and have failed in the attempt. As we stand within the King's Chamber, inhaling an 'atmosphere' that is nearly five thousand years old, I become almost petrified by the silence of the centuries. Outside the world moves on. Life roars on, without interval for rest or stillness. Here there is no movement. Centuries have come and gone, leaving no evidence of their passage within this hidden chamber. Five thousand years of time—five thousand years! The span of a single human life, what is it? Within these walls it seems as nothing. Civilisations, wars, human hopes and fears, life and death, all these shrink into insignificance. Yet nothing seems to take their place. One feels detached from the world of men and things, detached even from oneself, standing inert within a vacuum. Thousands visit the Great Pyramid each year, millions have been drawn into the desert since it first came into being, drawn by a strange and irresistible fascination. Can it be that this vacuum within an empty tomb has the power to cast a magic spell upon the restless souls of men? As I stand gazing down into the empty sarcophagus of Cheops, words from Laotzu come to my mind: 'Thirty spokes surround one wheel. The usefulness of the wheel is always in its empty innermost. You fashion clay to make a bowl, the usefulness of that bowl is always in its empty innermost. You cut out doors and windows to make a house; their usefulness to a house is always in their empty space. Therefore profit comes from external form, but usefulness comes from the empty innermost!'

What usefulness, I wonder, can come from the 'empty innermost' within this great pyramid, standing in the central desert of the earth?

There is no feeling of sanctity within this tomb, simply the sensation of complete emptiness. I remembered Private Dowding's words: 'Empty yourself of self if you would be filled', and begin to understand their meaning.

Should we make pilgrimage to the desert and penetrate to the empty centre of this monument that we may learn to understand the true significance of silence? Certainly when standing there one feels the uselessness of much that we call the activities of 'life'. Should one come here to pierce the veil between the world of illusion and the world of truth? The candle has gone out and we are plunged in darkness. I grope my way along the wall, seeking escape both from my thoughts and from this tomb....

And now we are outside again, bathed in the strong Egyptian sunlight.

I sit down on the hot yellow sand, exhausted by the long scramble through narrow and steep passages. We put on our coats and shoes and gaze away towards the river and the busy city beyond. It is as if the world were once more closing in around us, clamouring for our attention, reminding us that we are still subject to the phantasies of external living. Strange sensations are still surging through me. I feel as if the whole world—my whole world—had been standing still, while I lived back through five thousand years in the silent tomb we had just left. And now the machinery of life is again in motion. I am whirled back into the midst of noisy movements and events.

Surely these can never stir me to fear again, or to passion or tumultuous action? I sit gazing across the desert away towards a far-off mirage, wondering how far I have correctly caught the meaning of this majestic monument.

We move on towards the second pyramid, slightly smaller than the first, built by Chephren (known as the Pharaoh Khafra) some seventy years later than the Pyramid of Cheops. It is less impressive, built of inferior stone, and shows signs of dilapidation. We do not go inside, but pass on until we stand before the third (and smallest) of the Ghizeh pyramids, completed about 2800 B.C. as the tomb of Mycerinus, son of Khafra, grandson of the Great Cheops. On its eastern side the sand slopes away towards the Nile and it is here that the ruins of the temple, known as the Upper Temple of the Mycerinus Pyramid, were unearthed in 1906. Malaby Firth is now completely in his element. We spend much time in examining all that is left of what must once have been an impressive building. Each of the three pyramids is said to have had two temples attached, called the Upper Temple and the Valley Temple, but the sand has swallowed nearly everything. I stand spellbound before an enormous block of red granite weighing at least one hundred tons. These blocks were originally intended for 'facing' the lower slopes of the pyramids themselves. While examining this stone, I notice a neat inscription in red paint across one of its corners. So clear cut and fresh is this inscription that it might have been written yesterday. Firth stoops down and reads it for me. Simply these words: 'For the King's House in the Desert.' Probably a foreman at the Asswed quarries, over six hundred miles away, had labelled the stone thus some five thousand years ago.

'For the King's House in the Desert'! In those days there was only one king and one king's desert house, and so the stone could not go astray while it journeyed many hundreds of miles down the Nile on rafts.

Somehow this intimate human touch seems to bridge the centuries as in a lightning flash. In the King's Chamber of the Great Pyramid time had unrolled its way backwards, slowly, with halting ponderous steps. Out here in the sun, standing before this block of granite, gazing at a simple inscription, I felt immediately in touch with that quarry foreman as he bent down to label this great stone so that it should find its way safely to its rightful destination.

Why should we not each have a 'King's House' within the central desert of our being; a sanctuary where we could retire from storm and stress, where in the central stillness we could gain poise and strength and renew our faith? Perhaps after all I am only now beginning to understand the lesson of the pyramids!

We walk down a temple avenue towards the Sphinx. I notice that the floor is paved with slabs of alabaster. We pass out of the ruins and plod along across the sand.

The Sphinx is now in sight. As we approach it from behind, it looks like a giant mushroom throwing strange shadows across the ground. The sun is setting and the sands are empty. Here is a mystery indeed. I will not attempt to describe the indescribable. The Sphinx can be delineated as to its form and shape, but who can portray the thoughts and ideas that brought this creation into being? We pass on to the Temple of The Sphinx (also known as the Valley Temple of the second pyramid) and then turn round and sit down upon the sand. I will not speak of the Sphinx just now. I have often seen it before and I shall see it many times again. I will spend a night some time within the magic circle of its influence—a moonlight night. Then perhaps shall I feel able to speak out the thoughts that come to me. At present I am dumb before this mystery. I am still learning the lesson that is eternally waiting within the King's Chamber of the Great Pyramid to teach itself unto the minds of men: Silence, Stillness, Sanctuary; then the Summit.

> From the silence of time, time's silence borrow.
> In the heart of today is the WORD of tomorrow.
> The Builders of JOY are the children of sorrow.

Why should that triad of William Sharp's (written on an envelope and given to my sister at St. Bride's Well, Glastonbury, England, in 1908) refuse to leave my mind alone at such a moment? Have these great and most ancient monuments still some message for the future, waiting to be revealed? The world is certainly peopled with the children of sorrow. Are the Builders of Joy truly those who have learnt to become unselfed who spend much time in their own King's Chamber in the desert? 'Profit comes from external form, but usefulness from the empty innermost'. This is the final thought I take back with me from the desert, back with me into the world of war and woe. And, for me, it is a message of hope, of inspiration and of joy.

The Desert, The Khamsin and The Sphinx
(Written in March, 1918)

Today the desert called me with no uncertain voice. When the desert calls, there is profit in obedience. So I went out into the wild from the city on the Nile.

At Mena House I stopped awhile. It was a Sunday. The terrace before the hotel lies almost beneath the shadow of the Great Pyramid itself. A band was playing French airs, the terrace was crowded with English officers and their ladies. I sat down and ordered coffee; a long walk lay ahead, and my day had been a tiring one.

At the next table there sat two officers, down on leave from Palestine, and a well-known Egyptian Pasha. I could not help overhearing scraps of their conversation. The Pasha was speaking with animation and many gestures. Evidently the campaign north of the Jordan had been under discussion. 'You English are killing many Turks. Your nation has always professed friendship for the Moslem faith. Why are you killing Moslems up in Palestine?'

One of the officers, a captain, replied: 'Don't you see we must free the Holy Land from the Turkish yoke? Also we have to protect the road to India and the East. The British are not fighting a religious war in Palestine.'

The Pasha smiled. 'Then why are you turning out the Moslems in order to give the land to the Jews? Why hand over Palestine to the people who murdered your Christ Prophet so long ago? Does your religion mean so little to you?'

The captain had no reply available, but his companion spoke: 'We cannot throw stones at the Jews because their ancestors slew Jesus Christ. We have been murdering His teaching ever since. Few of us have the right to be called Christians.'

'Ah,' said the Pasha thoughtfully. 'If Moses, Mahomed and Jesus were in the world today, they would hold a council of peace, and there would be an end of war.'

This conversation rang in my ears as I set out for a long tramp across the desert. 'If Moses, Mahomed and Jesus were in the world today.' A strange phrase from the lips of a Moslem. The Pasha had spoken with conviction. His belief in the power of the prophets was evidently great. Can the prophets of the past stand idle now? Surely their voices will make themselves heard through the whirlwind of war and carnage. Out here in the wilderness perhaps they may be holding their council of peace.

The desert makes one think such thoughts. Have you ever walked on and on, hour after hour, until even the Great Pyramid vanishes from sight? This is what I did today. I was alone. There was no sign of life or movement. The sand seemed to undulate away towards the four corners of the earth. It is the period of the Khamsin, the Fifty Days' Wind, which sweeps across the desert every spring, heralding the approach of the summer heats. In the desert, where sand and sky alone are visible, wind assumes a new significance.

The Khamsin is the wind of winds. One can almost watch its approach, surging gently up out of the south, moulding its movements to the billowing sand. This wind has entity, intelligence, spirit. Today the Khamsin is a friend, I can speak with it while its gentle breezes blow around me. It holds a message which I strive hard to understand. It is a wind with which one can commune. But the Khamsin is not always in friendly mood. I have known it blow fiercely, lashing the cruel sand against one's face. Within an hour I may lie buried beneath the turbulence of a storm of sand. Then the Khamsin is one's enemy.

Today the sand lies quiet, the wind blows gently; the sun is not too hot, and all is well. There broods a Presence in the desert that I have never found elsewhere. Today I felt this Presence strongly. I have likened it before to an elemental mind. This mind fills the empty spaces of the world, and at times it gives of its abundance both to man and Nature.

The empty spaces both on land and sea have their special usefulness; of this I have now ceased to doubt.

The wind has dropped, the sun is dipping towards the west. Out of the sand a mist arises. This mist seems substanceless. One moment it is not, the next it fills all the vast spaces of the wilderness. This mist is warm, mysterious, golden-grey. It rises up between one's feet as if from the centre of the earth. It does not come *across* the desert sands, but rises from within them. I have known the Khamsin mist appear from nowhere and, almost instantly, cover all the spaces between the desert and the city on the Nile. Uncanny silences follow in its wake. The sun goes out. And so it was today, as I turned and wandered back towards the desert monuments. My mind was full of questioning. It often is out here: vague, searching questions that seem unanswerable. Perhaps the Sphinx has some message for me before the moon comes up. In Egypt one always turns towards the Sphinx when baffled by the mystery of the land. And yet, the Sphinx is the greatest mystery of all. Tonight the moon is not yet up, the mist has cleared, the stars above are radiant in blue.

The Sphinx at night! It is the wonder of the world. Travellers speak of it as an inscrutable monument hewn from rock, expression unchangeable. It is not this to me. I have never seen the same Sphinx twice. This is no simple carven image rising from the desert waste, gazing eternally towards the east. Let us sit down upon the sand awhile. Those eyes! What do they see? The mouth. Surely words lie behind it? Those ears. Are they not listening in the silence? Every curve of face and figure expresses power and life.

This image is more than a rock-hewn idol. It is a great symbol, and it is more. The Sphinx expresses life elemental, life that can be felt by all who stand before it. The questions I have come to ask die down upon my lips. Those eyes pierce into the recesses of my being, into the secret chamber, hidden within, where the answer to all questions can be found.

I begin to understand. I have brought *with me* the solution to every problem. There is no need to ask the Sphinx to unlock the gate of knowledge. All that I need to know, I know already. The Sphinx has one great message to proclaim to those who make pilgrimage to its feet. Tonight the message took this form: 'Cease searching in the outer world to solve the mystery of life. Within yourself there is a chamber. It lies hidden at the end of a long, winding corridor. This chamber is your secret sanctuary. There you will find all that is needed by your soul. Stay with me awhile in silence, and I will lead you to the door. The door is locked, but the key is in your hand. It has always been there, invisible, while you have ranged the wide world searching for it.

'Use your own key. Retire within. I will not come beyond the threshold. In showing you the way, my task is done.'

This is what the Sphinx said to me tonight. I believe it gives the same message, in a myriad ways, to each one who stands silently before it, listening.

The moon is rising across the river. The desert becomes a silver lake. The silence deepens. The message of the Sphinx is with me. The key is in my hand. I hasten down the corridor. I pass through many avenues within my mind. I stand before that inner door, key in hand. The door is open. Here is sanctuary at last. I have no need to seek elsewhere, for within the sanctuary I can see the light. Within the light, the prophets of God Omnipotent are walking. Peace dwells therein. I hear the Sphinx speak once more: 'Those who attain true inner peace become God's messengers in a world at war. Shed forth the light from your secret sanctuary until it is caught up and reflected everywhere. Then will a world at war become a world at peace.'

CHAPTER EIGHT

An Exercise in the Use of the Imagination

The notes recorded in the previous chapter were set down over forty years ago. The message which now follows was written in 1959 and should be regarded as a personal communication from the author to each reader of this book. Although the wording is very different, the theme is similar to that contained in the writings which precede it. As a result, the span of forty years ceases to exist and thus becomes a natural sequence of ideas as from one moment to the next.—W. T. P.

IN MY VIEW the faculty of creative imagination is one of our most valuable possessions. This faculty should not be confused with the phantasies evolved by the brain when acting independently of the mind. No masterpiece in any of the arts or in other fields of human endeavour could come to fruition if the gift of creative imagination were denied to man. There are ways in which the fruits of this gift can be enjoyed without the need for their manifestation in external form.

Let me give an example of what I mean.

The mind of man is a house of many mansions. We each possess one of our own.

Remember that yours will remain the habitation you are destined to use throughout your pilgrimage across eternity.

'Man, know thyself' is an injunction that has echoed down the centuries, but so far little progress seems to have been made in responding to this call. The key to self-knowledge is to be found within the mind and we should seek for it there and nowhere else. No key but yours will fit the lock of that inner gateway beyond which lies your own sanctuary of spiritual awareness. My key will not fit your lock, nor yours mine, for as has been said elsewhere, the search for truth is a solitary adventure. If you are ready to undertake this exploration seriously, why not summon to your aid the faculty of creative imagination? It is a gift from God, freely available for our use now and at all times.

Your house of many mansions is not built by hands. It is situated within yourself and is an essential and a permanent part of you. It is your citadel. Picture yourself standing within its portals and take conscious possession of your property.

Pass from room to room remembering that you have the power to furnish each of them to suit your tastes and needs. Continue your exploration until you reach the door leading to the sanctuary of your being. Realise that the key of entry is in your hand. Use it. Go in and close the door. Here you will find yourself at home. Treat this inner sanctuary with care and reverence. Regard the place where you now stand as holy ground, a temple of the spirit and a haven of rest from the turmoil of the outer world. Utilise the services of your imagination to create an altar before which to pray.

Now is the time to relieve your shoulders of the burdens they have been carrying, the problems that have weighed so heavily upon you, the tasks which hitherto have seemed beyond your ability to fulfil. Take these burdens and lay them upon the altar before which you kneel, remembering with thankfulness that 'the government is upon His shoulders'. We have the highest authority for permission to 'cast our burdens upon the Lord'. Then ask for that understanding which will enable you to become of greater service to your fellow men. Such service is the fulfilling of the law of Love. It is the Holy Grail of all endeavour. Request nothing for yourself because in the fulfilling of the law 'all these things shall be added unto you'. Then rest awhile in the silence of complete stillness. When you leave this inner shrine, lock the door behind you but take the key and keep it in safe custody. The time will come when, once having found and used this key, you will return more and more often to this hallowed place.

Make a habit of preparing yourself to do so before retiring each evening. In due course the journey will become a joyful and familiar pilgrimage. As a result the perplexities that beset you in the outer world of men and matters will begin to fall away. Life will assume a new and joyful guise. Fears and anxieties for yourself or others will disappear, for you will have brought light into your consciousness and you will be at rest. At rest, yes, but able from then onward to bring illumination to those who sit in darkness and so help them on their way towards that peace and understanding which you have found. Soon now you will be ready to take another and important forward step. The occasion will arise when you will feel impelled to assume once more those burdens which you had laid upon the altar. And behold! they will have ceased to weigh you down and will have become transmuted into opportunities of achievement. You will be following what is known as the 'Pathway of Relinquishment and Reassumption' and you will be wise to think out for yourself the significance of what this means.

From now onwards you will not be alone. A Companion will have joined you to guide your footsteps forward. He will help you to understand that the key to the best solution of every human problem lies within the problem itself and not outside it.

The task of discovering this solution will now be easier, but do not be disturbed if the upshot does not always turn out to be in accordance with your hopes and expectations. This is of no consequence because that which you had relinquished and which you have now reassumed is no longer something to be feared. It has become instead a stepping-stone in your climb towards fulfilment. Your enemy has become your friend and this friend has brought into your life a Companion to be your guide and comforter.

It will have become clear that the 'laying down' and the 'taking up' process described above has in no way involved the shirking of your mundane responsibilities meanwhile. You will now realise that it is not these responsibilities themselves which have constituted the burden but the fears that you had infused into them; the anxiety as to your ability to fulfil them satisfactorily.

It is the weight of *this* burden that will now have been removed, thereby enabling you to go forward on your way rejoicing.

. . . . .

In the above allegory I have tried to suggest a means by which constructive imagery used prayerfully with the right motives can become a gateway to reality. The particular form of spiritual alchemy which has made this transmutation possible will be discussed elsewhere.

I should be glad to think that the simple method of initiation outlined above may prove of as much service to you as it has been to me. It is one of the ways through which realisation is reached that 'the Kingdom of Heaven is within you' and not in some distant region beyond our present recognition and attainment.

CHAPTER NINE

Food for Thought

I HAVE BEEN asked to include the five short essays which form this chapter although they have already appeared privately in pamphlet form.

On Meditation

The practice of meditation is subject to law in the same way that mathematics or any other science is subject to law.

Meditation bears little good fruit until we have learned how to control our thoughts and feelings in order to bring about an interior stillness of mind. True meditation consists in communion with spirit leading to a clear realisation of the presence of God within one's whole being. It is useless to try to meditate simply by emptying the mind or by allowing one's thoughts to drift first in one direction and then in another. Meditation must be based on a principle, that is to say on a firm foundation supplied by a clear realisation of a basic truth. Otherwise our human thoughts and feelings, our hopes and fears, our physical condition of health or disease will dominate the mind and render all attempts at meditation fruitless.

Brother Lawrence, in his writings, lays down some simple rules for meditation, by which word he means the practice of the Presence of God. The principle upon which he founded his meditations was embodied in the firm conviction and clear realisation that Divine Love is a power and a presence that is always and immediately available for use within the consciousness of each one of us. We have here indeed a very secure foundation upon which to base our exercise of the services of meditation both for our own and for other people's welfare. To try to meditate without a principle of guidance is powerless to produce satisfactory results.

Here are a few simple rules which I have found useful as a preliminary to the practice of meditation.

Retire into your own room where you can be free from noise and distraction. Sit upright but in a comfortable chair and be careful to see that neither the light nor its reflection is strongly impinging upon your vision, otherwise there is risk of producing an hypnotic condition of mind. Meditation should not take place in complete darkness. No ticking clock should be in the room. After a few minutes' complete stillness it is well to focus your mind on the *object* and reason for your meditation and then allow intuition or interior perception to convey to you the most suitable *principle* upon which to base your meditationary period. There are those who find it helpful to read a short passage of Scripture (like the 91st Psalm) as a means for quietening the outer senses and for creating a measure of tranquillity. You may care to dwell upon the parable which indicates that God is not to be found in the strong wind nor in the earthquake nor in the fire but only within the silence of the still small voice.

Having tranquillised your thoughts and feelings, shutting out all material preoccupations, it is good to spend a few minutes in the practice of deep, natural rhythmic breathing.

At this point it is as well to state (to yourself) the particular objective for your meditation, sending up a prayer that you may become attuned to the spirit of all love and truth.

Now the time has arrived to *stop thinking thoughts* and to realise yourself as being within the light of God's Presence, humble, receptive and serene. From this point onwards, no instructions or directions given by one person to another can be of any real value, because your own soul will take charge and no external aids can apply.

A period of meditation should always end by offering a prayer of thankfulness and gratitude to God, followed by a gradual return to the normal conditions of daily life.

There are some who find help in the use of symbols in connection with their times of meditation.

As an instance, consider for a moment the significance of the symbolism contained in the circle, the cross and the cup. The circle, as a sun sign represents the Light of the all-pervading presence of God, within which we live and move and have our being. Here in itself is a valuable principle of truth on which to base a whole series of periods of meditation. The cross as a symbol of duality, of the descent from spirit into matter is also the symbol of redemption through Christ and of the Ascension through discipline and suffering resulting in a return from matter into spirit.

The cup or chalice is the symbol of the uprising from the duality of the cross to the unity on which all God's creation is based, the ultimate goal of human endeavour. It is the symbol containing the wine of inspiration, a fount ever flowing and available to us all through which the ideal of the Brotherhood of Man under the Fatherhood of God can become an actuality. In this particular form of meditation, we can picture the circle, ablaze with light and containing within itself the symbol of the cross, gradually dissolving to reveal the golden chalice filled with rose red wine, the veritable Holy Grail and the central symbol for the coming age.

One last point: before a meditation begins, cast out all personal desires, fears or hopes, all sense of dread perplexity or frustration. Adopt the humble attitude of one who says 'Here am I. Send me' and entrust your entire being to the arms of the sustaining Infinite.

· · · · ·

The Gift of Giving

Most people are taught to accept that the main objective in life is to get and to hold, without any question arising of the need to give in return. As a result, the law of love is violated with consequences that are only too apparent on every side.

Those who give freely all that is within their power to give will find that their own needs are always met. To give in the spirit of selflessness is to get, but to attempt to get without giving is surely contrary to Divine law and can bring no lasting satisfaction. I think it can be safely said that the working of this law is as applicable to nations as it is to individuals. Nearly all world problems could be solved by an understanding of the principles involved in giving and in the giving of thanks.

The following illustration has been used before, but it is very apt:

There are two seas in Palestine. One is filled with fresh and sparkling water. Trees and flowers grow around it. Fish live in it and its banks are green. The pure waters of this sea, which possess a healing quality, are brought down by the river Jordan from the hills around Mount Hermon. The Master loved this sea and many of the happier moments of His ministry were spent beside it. It is a place filled to this day with serenity and power.

The river Jordan flows on south into another sea.

Here there is no life, no song of birds, no children's laughter. The air hangs sinister and heavy above its water and neither man nor beast nor bird will drink. This sea is dead.

What makes so mighty a difference between these two seas of Palestine?

This is the difference—the Sea of Galilee receives but does not keep the waters of the Jordan. For every drop that flows into it another drop flows out. The more it gives joyfully away the more it receives in return. This is the Sea of Life.

The other sea hoards every drop of water reaching it and gives nothing in return. The Sea of Galilee gives and lives. The other sea gives nothing and does not live. It is truly named 'The Dead'.

It seems to me that to give and to give thanks will open many doors that would otherwise remain barred against us.

Jesus gave thanks and blessed the five barley loaves and the two small fishes in the sure knowledge that as a consequence the Divine law of supply would be brought into operation. He gave thanks to His Father *before* the manifestation had taken place and abundance followed as a natural sequence. It is easy to give thanks after a blessing has been received, although we often forget to do so. It is not so easy to give thanks when everything looks black and the problem facing us seems to be insoluble. Surely this is the thanks that counts because it flows from a faith which understands the working of the law of love.

Is it not well worth while to observe the Silent Minute at nine each evening in the spirit of thankfulness that seeks no reward beyond the joy of giving?

There are those who use the Minute to ask for strength and courage to meet and solve their own personal problems and perplexities.

There are those who use the Minute to link themselves in thought and prayer with absent relatives and friends or with loved ones who are no longer here.

Many keep the Minute in prayer for the nation's leaders, for understanding between the peoples, and for the coming of universal fellowship and peace.

Then there are others who remain silent and receptive, listening for the still small voice of guidance and inspiration.

An increasing number use this simple prayer: 'May Thy will be done on earth. Show me how to do my part,' and then remain quietly still, knowing that opportunities of service will come to them in God's own way and time.

Complete uniformity of method in keeping the Minute is not to be expected, but it is hoped that a bond of fellowship may invisibly unite all who meet in silence at nine each evening. What I would like to suggest is that we should agree to keep what for many is the most important moment of the day in the spirit of thankfulness. By this I do not mean to suggest that Remembrance and Resolve, the other two watchwords that have been chosen for the Minute, should be absent from our thoughts, but simply that thanksgiving should be the predominating keynote of the observance.

To give and to give thanks, in the increasing recognition of Christ's presence in our midst, will fulfil the law and bring us happiness and peace.

. . . . .

To One Bereaved

Notes based on a letter to a correspondent who lost her husband and two sons in a motor accident.

You tell me that your belief in an after-life is very firm and that you have read many books on the subject of after-death conditions. But that the more you read, the more confused does your mind become. You ask for some simple description of the relation of physical death to the hereafter.

I am not an authority on this subject and can only tell you the result of my own researches and experiences along these lines. Firstly, I think it is important to remember all the time that what we think of as 'death' contains within itself a birth or a renewal of life in the conditions of a wider state of consciousness or of awareness. At death we throw aside the mantle of our bodily form, but we throw off nothing else which belongs to us or is a part of us. Whilst alive on earth our spirit (that is the real and eternal self, individual, indestructible) is clothed within the soul, the soul is clothed within the mind, the mind is clothed (for the time being) in the physical body. This physical body is surrounded by what is sometimes called an etheric mould or semi-invisible counterpart. This mould has certain functions to perform as an intermediary between the body and the soul. After the body has disintegrated, it gradually disappears, there being no further use for its services. What happens at death is the withdrawal of spirit, soul and mind, as a trinity, from their earthly form and from external manifestation in the three-dimensional world of life and being.

Whilst on earth the spirit, soul and mind, although part of one whole or entity, are rarely fully active.

The 'nature life' which infuses our bodily form takes prior place in most of our activities on earth, but this nature life is not individual to ourselves but is the common property of all forms of 'life' manifesting in this our present world. At death the only part of us that 'dies' (for us) is this nature life or physical vitality followed by the disintegration of the bodily form which contains it. The value of the experiences garnered through the use of the nature life just referred to becomes the property of the soul and is taken forward into the next life for use in new conditions.

To the completely unevolved man still hardly conscious except in an animal and instinctive sense, death must really seem to be the end of all things, but his embryonic spirit, mind and soul are well looked after when he 'passes on', and we need not concern ourselves with this problem here.

In this connection I often think we should do well occasionally to stop and think about what we shall be leaving behind us when we go from here. I am not, of course, referring to material possessions but to other legacies that, inevitably, we shall bequeath to present and future generations.

Firstly there will be the effect of all our thoughts, words and deeds, that is to say their cumulative effect for good or ill on human consciousness as a whole: no small matter indeed. Then there is the legacy of the 'nature life' referred to above, which has infused vitality into our earthly form from birth to death. We can return this 'life' to the general reservoir, either enriched by the good use we have made of it, or tainted by the manner in which we have misused it whilst it has been in our possession. These are matters that call for deep meditation, it seems to me, and for right action before it is too late to act at all.

Now we come to something that is almost impossible to explain; namely, what it means to pass at death out of a three- into a four-dimensional state of being. Our language is three-dimensional, and so it is impossible to use words to explain what is meant by a state of living, to which one more dimension has been added. It is true I think to say that our thoughts (and certainly our dreams) 'operate' in four and not in only three dimensions—and it is also true to say that the addition of this further dimension to our experience of living and being has the effect of destroying for us the bondage of 'form', 'time' and 'space' conditions. Whilst on earth, it is as if we were in a cage, unable to get outside, whereas this cage disappears at 'death' and gives us a freedom that passes our present understanding altogether.

When we are born into this world it is necessary to learn, step by step, how to see and feel and think, and how to move our limbs and eat our food and how to master all the bodily activities.

When we 'die' and are immediately born into a new habitation, a very similar process takes place. For a time, varying in length according to the spiritual and moral development of the individual concerned, we remain asleep, or quiescent and unthinking, in preparation for the next step. It is true that after sudden death and in certain other cases there is a flash of complete consciousness immediately after the 'passing' experience; but usually this is not of long duration.

For a highly evolved soul no period of sleep or quiescence following physical death is necessary.

It should never be forgotten that when we awake into our new surroundings, we are exactly as we were before in so far as our thoughts and feelings and general make-up are concerned. Any changes that take place as we grow accustomed to our new habitation are gradual, but we never lose our complete sense of individuality.

I might tell you something here about those beings who are known as the Angels of the Passing. These are not angels in a celestial sense, but human beings who are very advanced in their development and who have elected to return to what is sometimes termed the borderland region which lies just beyond the frontiers of our present earthly realm. The duties of these beings are very beautiful to consider and to watch—their activities are somewhat similar to those of a midwife in that they help each soul to leave its earthly form in an orderly manner and to emerge unscathed into the wider life that is encompassed by four-dimensional conditions instead of three. The Angels of the Passing superintend the severing of the silver cord and help to free you and me (when our time comes) from our present prison house.

Another of their tasks is to call for the help of relatives or friends of the soul who is being born into the new state of consciousness, that is to say relatives or friends or loved ones who have already experienced physical death, and who are at home in their new surroundings. When, for instance, your husband or your sons awakened into their new life, they were 'met' by people whom they already knew and loved, and so were soon freed from any sense of fear or loneliness. You ask me to give you details of what life is like in borderland and in the wider world above it, but this is a big task, perhaps an impossible one, because we have no language capable of describing such conditions. What is important, as I said before, is to regard death as birth, as a new and glorious rebeginning and not as an abrupt end without a sequel. It is a completely natural process and it should be the custom to rejoice when death releases a loved one into a freedom and a happiness that are quite unknown to us whilst still on earth. Sorrow and regret for them or for ourselves is quite out of place; just as much so as it would be foolish to regret the throwing away of an overcoat when it was worn out and beyond repair.

You will ask why it is that so many 'overcoats' have to be discarded before they are worn out—this is a very important question involving the twin laws of love and justice operating in close connection with the law of cause and effect as established over long periods of existence and on many occasions, both here and in other worlds of life and being. Divine Love is fulfilled in justice and we need never fear the result, even if for the time being we may not be able to understand how these laws work.

And so when sorrow seems to overwhelm you, keep

on saying to yourself: 'Death is the joyful gateway to a new and wider life, and I rejoice in the freedom that has now come to my beloved ones.'

· · · · ·

Affluence

What a lovely word this is and yet in its full significance how little understood! Contrary to common belief true affluence does not consist in a large bank balance or the possession of houses, property or motor-cars. Such material amenities may represent outer reflections of 'supply' but affluence itself is a divine gift within the reach of those who care to learn how to become receptive to this gift and worthy to possess it. We speak of 'the Infinite Love of God' towards all the beings that He has created but rarely do we stop to consider the full meaning of this stupendous statement. Nor do we often realise that the out-pouring of infinite love must include affluence among its gifts. In fact we cannot imagine one without the other.

Life itself is free, we do not have to buy it, nor do we buy the capacity to think and to feel. These possessions belong to us as surely as the very air we breathe. Affluence in the true meaning of the word is available to us now and always. It is a gift of the spirit and its origin is never mundane. Even if this statement seems to be too transcendental for our present acceptance, pause a moment to give it careful thought before you reject its implications altogether.

There is nothing visible in man's life on earth that did not originate as an 'idea'. The house you live in, the car you drive, the business which occupies you, the very table at which I am now writing came into being from an idea or from a combination of ideas. This of course is only another way for saying that the material universe as we know it has a mental origin. Ideas cannot be created by what we call physical substance. They are children of the mind and the mind's capacity to think is a gift 'beyond price' which is our common heritage. It is in fact a truism to say not only that 'thoughts are things' but that no 'thing' can come into existence without a thought behind it.

Among God's gifts to man is the possession of free will. Consequently we are at liberty to align our thinking with the Source of our being, which inevitably results in affluence, or we can refuse to do so which results sooner or later in a sense of poverty and lack. The choice is ours and it is a choice which is renewable from day to day.

The average man, if the question be put to him, will assert that all he needs and longs for here and now is good health, happiness, friends and enough money to live on amply. His attention is concentrated not on ideas but on their external outcome in the form of 'things' and conditions, the possession of which appears to him to depend almost entirely on the contents of his purse. Such an attitude of mind makes it impossible to tap the Source of affluence and to ensure its never failing bounty. If you tell such a man that his well-being in every sense of the word depends solely upon his attitude of mind, he will dismiss this suggestion with incredulity, yet it happens to be true!

The Cosmos itself was created by an Idea sometimes referred to as the Logos or Word of God. The spirit of each one of us is a reflection of this Cosmos and an infinite supply of ideas is ever flowing into the orbit of our minds. We have the power to obstruct this flow or to take advantage of it. We also have the power to combine such ideas in harmonious sequence or to misuse them or even to refuse their entrance altogether. As a result, affluence (or its lack) does not depend upon people, or circumstances beyond our control, which we are only too ready to believe, but upon our attitude of mind and the way in which we use ideas. If one tries to state this truth in metaphysical terms, it would be accurate to say that our affluence and general well-being will inevitably increase, through prayer and right motives, in direct proportion to our efforts to align our thinking with the Source of Life itself. 'In Him we live and move and have our being' can be as true for us today as it ever will be, for in the Mind of God, our Father, there is no 'time' that must be endured. There is instead the eternal and ever-present NOW.

· · · · ·

Thinking from the Summit

Perhaps it is natural that we should tend to identify ourselves almost exclusively with the physical body. We incline to give it reality as an integral part of the '*I am*' within, instead of regarding it as a temporary garment, which is shed when no longer of further use to us.

A neighbour who called to tell me about the loss of her mother said, 'I have lost my dear one. She is dead.' When I pointed out the fact that it was only her mother's physical body and not her mother who was dead, she replied, 'I cannot recognise the difference.' This situation is very common.

A great deal of unnecessary suffering resulting from a sense of separation comes from the habit ingrained in many people of regarding the physical body as being the real you or me. In this and indeed in all other connections, the word *death* as meaning a final and extinguishing end should be expunged from our dictionaries! It should be replaced by the word 'separation' from the physical which in fact is the only true meaning of the term *death*, as exemplified by the departure of life from the form it has temporarily used.

Recently a friend came in for a chat. After a while he

said, 'What a lovely day it is! Let us take our bodies out for a walk. The exercise will do them good.'

This remark struck me as a right step forward in helping to change the direction of my thinking. It made one realise how unwisely one has fallen into the habit of identifying oneself almost exclusively with the form in which one is temporarily housed. It is useful sometimes when saying, 'I am going to do so and so', to stop and ask oneself whether one is referring to the body or to one's real self. Or to some combination of both as if they were an indissoluble whole.

To cease identifying oneself exclusively with the physical body as the real you or me does not mean that its temporary possession is valueless.

A garment is useful so long as it is kept in good condition. That the body has a nature life which is available for our present use, of course cannot and should not be overlooked. But the more I identify myself with it, as being me, the more insistent will become its demand for undivided and exclusive attention, sometimes as a result, making foolish and unwarranted claims upon me who am but its wearer.

Have you ever considered the value of starting your thinking from the summit of your understanding and descending from there rather than the other way about? The mode of 'thinking from the body' upwards often ends in a return of one's thoughts to the needs and claims of the body to the exclusion of all else.

'I am so tired', or 'I feel ill and I am in pain', may echo in my thinking to such an extent as to make me forget it is the body claiming to be me taking advantage of my passive consent to identification with it.

Let us see how the good habit of 'thinking from the summit' can be developed.

Let us try to lift up our thought, in prayer and meditation to the point of First Departure, to the source of our being, in fact to the Creator.

One way of drawing near to God is through a consideration of His attributes.

Therefore if we think of Him as being infinite *life*, *love* and *wisdom*, we are approaching as closely as is humanly possible to the 'point of our First Departure'. If this is so, then our first task should be to meditate very carefully on the meaning of the word 'infinite'—perhaps the most awe-inspiring word in the language.

A good but by no means adequate definition of the word 'infinite' is: 'Limitless as to duration, boundless as to space and wholly inexhaustible.'

The next useful step in our effort to 'think from the summit' is to apply this definition to the best of our ability to the meaning of the words 'life', 'love' and 'wisdom' and to ponder on the significance of such an application.

Your and my conceptions of the true significance of the ideas signposted by these great words may be frail and faulty. This fact should not deter us because we are in the process of replacing the bad habit of beginning our thinking from the basement by the good habit of starting from the roof-top. Perhaps I can best explain what I am trying to describe by an allegory. In any case this presents a worth-while foundation for meditation upon the true significance of the 'I am', which is the real you and me:

The Creator of the Universe plants a seed in the spiritual soil of Heaven. This seed grows up. It is you. In due course three gifts are offered to you by the Deity: (1) The gift of eternal life; (2) the gift of intelligence or mind; (3) the gift of the capacity to draw upon the inexhaustible resources of Life, Love and Wisdom.

The primary use to which you could put the gift of intelligence when responding to the Divine declaration: 'Because I am, Thou art' is by replying 'Because God is, I am'—'In Him I live and move and have my being'. This is Christ's teaching.

What a complete change of outlook this involves compared with the mundane habit of thinking and believing that 'I live and move and have my being' exclusively in my physical body!

Remember that you draw your very being from the eternal fountain of Life, your very being in God. From the wellspring of love in order to reflect His love in fellowship and service to others. From the source of wisdom in order to understand the purpose of your life and to fulfil it.

To continue the allegory. You, having become living and spiritual, must needs go forth upon your Father's business. Inevitably you will require a form in which to do this.

You therefore become clothed by the Grace of God in a garment which is your spiritual body. This garment being made of spiritual substance is indestructible, perfect and free from the dangers of decay. It is your real body which never changes but which may wear outer garments or 'bodies' which your spiritual identity uses in service when required.

In the terms of this attempt allegorically to state a great truth, the 'I am', your spiritual self, lives in the Mind, the Consciousness which is God, not only in some far-distant future, but here and always. You and I can think, speak and act from this standpoint, *now*, even whilst apparently hindered by the present veils of flesh surrounding us.

You and I have the right to declare eternally 'I am spiritual and I worship God in Spirit and in truth'.

You may wonder what the value of such a complete change in your thinking as I have tried to describe may turn out to be. The full reply to this question is not for me to give, but in any case a stilling of the outer self in order that we may learn how to be 'absent from the body and present with the Lord' eases both mental and physical tensions and thus becomes an effective healing exercise.

Apart from this undoubted benefit I can only suggest that it may be worth your while to make such a method the basis for your prayers and for your periods of meditation.

It will not be easy at first. Experience shows that persistent effort is essential before valuable results can be expected. On waking in the morning, begin by reaching up in thought towards the summit of your understanding. During the day, whenever you begin a new train of thought, start at the top. When faced by a problem rise above it and look down upon it. Refuse to descend to the point where you would become merged in the perplexities of the problem and so lose the right perspective for solving it.

And when you are preparing to keep the Silent Minute at nine o'clock each evening bring back to mind what has already been written in these notes. Meditate awhile quietly on the *meaning* of:

> Here and now I draw from the fountain of Life to manifest my existence in God. From the wellspring of Love so that I reflect His Love in fellowship and service to others.
>
> From the source of Wisdom in order to understand the purpose of my life and to fulfil it.

The time will come both for you and for me, when as a result, a deep silence will descend upon us, a silent stillness filled with the love of God.

And out of this silence a still small voice will make itself heard and the answer we seek will be both yours and mine.

When this happens how wonderful it will be to go our ways rejoicing and to be at peace!

CHAPTER TEN

Light out of Darkness

THE TRADITIONAL STORY of Lucifer, Prince of Darkness, as it has reached us from a very ancient past, is without parallel in its range of interest and of paradox. 'How art thou fallen from Heaven, O Lucifer (Day-star), Son of the Morning?' This question put by the prophet Isaiah might well be rendered in this way: In what manner and for what reason art thou fallen from Heaven, O Lucifer, whilst still retaining your heavenly titles of Day-star and Son of the Morning? It is to be noted that even when Lucifer is traditionally associated with 'Satan' or the Prince of Darkness, he is still referred to as the Light-bringer and the Shining One. Is there some clue here to the mystery of how light can emerge from darkness, how what we call 'evil' can be transmuted into good? Just as we are given in the early chapters of Genesis two widely different accounts of Creation,* so two entirely distinct stories concerning Lucifer and his fall, have come down to us. The more orthodox of the two relates how Lucifer, originally an angel of great light, rebelled against his Creator and was banished from the

---

* The first account is given in Genesis i. and up to ii. 5 inclusive. The second account begins Genesis ii. 6: 'And there went up a mist from the earth.'

heavenly spheres. He was therefore forced to descend into our world and the underworld, ultimately to become identified in Biblical records with Satan and also with Diabolos, the Accuser and the Calumniator. An earlier tradition of Lucifer's 'fall' from grace is more subtle in its implications and may be a nearer approximation to the truth. . . . Lucifer, one of the Seven Angels around the throne of the Creator of the solar universe, was reputed to be the guardian of the sacred planet Venus,* one that is said to be far higher in the spiritual scale of evolution than our own world. A time came when God called for a volunteer from amongst His angels, one who was willing to descend into the material darkness of human consciousness on earth. This angel was asked to sacrifice himself by undertaking his new mission veiled as the Prince of Darkness. The tradition goes that Lucifer responded to his Father's call, and sacrificing his high estate, 'fell' or descended into matter and so came to dwell in our midst, becoming known among us as 'Satan' or the Adversary (but not necessarily an evil being).

In Revelation, St. John tells us of a star (Angel) who fell from Heaven, and to whom was given the key of the bottomless pit (Rev. ix. 1), a reference which might well apply to Lucifer himself, who according to an early record was given keys of the Underworld and the control of the forces of Nature.

To continue the allegory. . . . When Lucifer entered human conditions, he is said to have met with no response to his willingness to become the Lightbringer, and owing to the ignorance and opposition of mankind the light of his Star became dimmed amidst

---

* This radiant star has been the first to be noticed since earliest ages; it is the only planet mentioned by Homer: Isaiah celebrates her splendour under the name of Lucifer; at the time of the pyramids the Egyptians called her 'the celestial bird of morn'; thirty-five centuries ago the Babylonians observed one of its transits across the sun; the Indians called her 'the brilliant', and the Arabs 'Zorah, the splendour of the sky'. Camille Flammarion, *Dream of an Astronomer*, page 95.

the dark conflicts that raged on earth. As Job has it (xxxviii): 'Where wast thou when I laid the foundations of the earth? Declare if thou hast understanding. . . . When the morning stars sang together [that is, before the descent of Lucifer, the Day-star from on high], and all the Sons of God shouted for joy. . . . Hast thou commanded the morning since thy days and caused the *Dayspring* to know his place? That it [he] might take hold of the ends of the earth that the wicked might be shaken out of it' (i.e., That the earth might be cleansed of sin). And so it came about that Lucifer's mission was not welcomed or understood by the sons of men. The methods he employed were such that he became erroneously known and feared as the Red Fiery Dragon or the Great Serpent, and as is always the case fear brought its own retribution, shrouding men's minds from the light. Lucifer in fact became the Tempter (the Tester) and the Redeemer in one. He taught and disciplined humanity (and still does so) by the provision of pains and sufferings through which mankind may be gradually stimulated and encouraged to turn away from the darkness of ignorance toward the light of understanding. . . . So runs this ancient allegory of Lucifer's mission to humanity, and who would care to deny that the story may well contain important elements of truth? Just as the human intellect would not know how to perceive light had it not experienced darkness, so Lucifer the Prince of Darkness brings to us the knowledge of the light. In this sense Christ and Lucifer may well be not only complementary one to the other, but also integral parts of the same whole. The promise in Revelation (ii. 28) seems to confirm this suggestion: 'And I will give him [i.e., he that overcometh] the morning star', a recognisable synonym for Lucifer, the Day-star and Son of the Morning.

It is surely true to say the light cannot be perceived without presupposing the existence of darkness, just as sound would have no significance if silence were nonexistent? Perhaps it would be equally true to say that were it not for the help of Lucifer, the Prince of Darkness, we should be incapable of discerning Christ, the Prince of Light? If Lucifer correctly interpreted is in fact complementary to the Christ, then a passage in II Peter (i. 19) takes on a deeper meaning: 'We have also a more sure word of prophecy whereunto ye do well that ye take heed as unto a light that shineth in a dark place until the day dawn [the realisation of the Christ presence] and the *day-star* [Lucifer] arise in your hearts.' In this connection it is not without interest to note that the morning star heralds the dawn of the greater light of the sun and is absorbed in it as the sun rises towards its full splendour.

It would seem as if our conception of Lucifer as a fearsome and evil entity is mistaken because he may well be as much an instrument of Divine purposes as Christ Himself (Rev. xxii. 16): 'I, Jesus, have sent *mine angel* to testify unto you these things. I am the bright and morning star.' Lucifer incarnated in human consciousness, and regarded as a kind of celestial leaven, can only arise and go to his Father in Heaven as humanity itself arises and progresses in the same direction. To regain his place in the spiritual realms, Lucifer must bring us with him, hence the references to this great being in eastern scripts as both the Tempter and Redeemer.

Perhaps it might be of interest here to give a list of the many names and titles by which Lucifer was known to the Ancients, and including those which have been mentioned already. Its range and variety are amazing: Lucifer, Prince of Darkness, Venus, Son of the Morning, Day-star or Day-spring from on high, the Dawnbringer, the Shining One, the Light-bringer, the Red Fiery Dragon, Phosphoros, the Prodigal Son, the Great Serpent, Tempter and Redeemer, Satan and the 'Evil

One', The Tester, Possessor of the Keys of the Dead, the Liberator, the Revealer, the Dweller on the Threshold, and the Intervener. In fact, Lucifer is the one word in the dictionary which combines the two extremes of the human conception of good and evil.

It is not without importance to emphasise once more that, so far as tradition can be relied upon, Lucifer was allowed to retain his celestial titles, even after his so-called 'fall' from Heaven. Does not this suggest that he descended from his high estate not as a rebel, who had been expelled for his evil deeds, but in order to undertake a great mission involving heavy sacrifice and by God's command? Is it not possible that St. Luke (Lucas—the luminous one) may have had this in mind as well as the more direct implication, when he wrote (i. 78): 'Through the tender mercies of our God, whereby the dayspring [or day-star] from on high hath visited us. To give light to them that sit in darkness and in the shadow of death and to guide our feet into the way of peace.' Is it to be Lucifer, the selfless sharer of our darkness, whose hand will lead us out into the Light, through the agency of the many trials and tribulations *he himself* imposes upon us; and when in that Light, we shall come to recognise Lucifer as indeed our Morning Star, the Dayspring from on high?

Somewhere it is written in an ancient Eastern text: 'And now it stands proven that Satan,* the Red Fiery Dragon, the Lucifer or Lightbearer *is in us*; 'It is our Mind, our Tempter and Redeemer, our Liberator and our Saviour from pure animalism.' If this statement is true, then there should be brotherly relations between Christ and Lucifer. They must be symbolically speaking, opposite sides of the same coin, because in

---

* The word 'Satan' is not here to be understood in the later sense of the enemy of man and God. The Satan is that one of God's ministers whose part is to oppose men in their pretensions to a right standing before God (Zechariah iii, 1); that is, who represents God's trying, sifting providence. A. G. Hogg, *The Message of the Kingdom*, page 26.

the ultimate sense, Absolute Light and Absolute Darkness must surely contain one another.

There is no doubt that Biblical commentators have confused the two allegories to which reference has been made. It is also true that Biblical records themselves have tried to blend into one story the two distinct accounts of the Lucifer mystery as is evidenced by the contradictory qualities that are attributed to this enigmatical being. I want to make it clear that in speaking of Lucifer as the herald of Christ the Eternal, I am referring to him on the basis of the earlier tradition only. This being the case, I reject the later interpolations which attempt to identify Lucifer with the Devil and all that is evil. Abaddon, the Appolyon of the Greeks, the destroyer, is according to this view a conception which is entirely distinct from Lucifer the Light-bringer, or even Satan (the Adversary). It will be remembered that in Job (i.), Satan is referred to as one who holds friendly converse with the Deity among those who are called the Sons of God. This is one of the Biblical instances when it would appear that Satan was entrusted with a Divine Mission, in this case as the tester of Job's faith and goodness. Job passes through the refiner's fire, the Luciferian flame, and as a result is given strength to overcome every calamity by which Satan besets him.

. . . . .

Having tried to tell the story of Lucifer, so far as it is possible to piece it together from the very scanty records available, it remains to be discovered whether there are any useful lessons to be learnt from this allegory, lessons that can be of practical service in our daily lives. There are those who will prefer to draw their own conclusions, but I will give a few reflections that have proved useful to me personally. . . . In our present state of knowledge, what we term good and evil, light and darkness, Christ and Lucifer, can only be defined and understood in a relative sense. . . . The main value of the Lucifer tradition as understood in its deeper meaning seems to lie in the extent to which his testing and revealing mission lifts humanity out of darkness into the light of Christ's redemptive and healing presence.... Our fear of what we call Satan appears to be the result of ignorance, and ignorance is the main cause of 'sin'. If what we term evil Intelligences exist in a fallen state of being, then every effort we make as individuals to lift ourselves up toward the Light, must help 'Satan' to redeem himself and so gradually to annul the consequences of the 'Fall from grace'. . . .* We should not fear Lucifer, the Liberator within ourselves, but co-operate with him by resisting the tests and temptations he puts before us and by understanding his role in the great Plan. . . . The production of electric current depends upon the friction of opposites—No ship or airplane could move forward unless the propellers met with the 'opposition' of sea or air, that is to say the contrary pressure of these media.

Is it not reasonable to apply this analogy to human progress and so to explain the value and rationale of Lucifer's opposition to man's upward striving towards the light?

In our daily lives each one can become either a light-bearer or a disseminator of darkness, having been given freewill to choose which path he will follow. (Light and Darkness are used here in their deeper sense, that is Light as wisdom or spiritual knowledge and Darkness as ignorance and selfishness). The process of being tested (tempted) is not in itself a sin. Temptations if resisted are instruments of progress, valuable opportunities for man to exercise his spiritual muscles. This is only another way for saying that the presence of Lucifer in human consciousness is a blessing (even if seemingly 'in

---

* Fear of death and hell seem to be man-made beliefs without any real foundation. Physical death is the gateway toward a wider and fuller life. It is probable that the only hell that exists resides in men's minds and has no reality outside human consciousness.

disguise' to us) and by no means something evil of which to be afraid. Our 'friend the enemy' (Lucifer) should be welcomed and not spurned, because all obstacles and difficulties placed in our way by him are intended to teach us how to rise through overcoming them. . . . Just as we are taught to pray for our enemies, so we should pray for the Lucifer who is imprisoned within us and who can only rise and return unto his Father as we do the same.

. . . . .

In *The Secret of Time and Satan* Edward Carpenter goes to the heart of the matter and puts the issue far better than I can. Here is what he says: 'And so at last I saw Satan appear before me . . . magnificent, fully formed. . . . Feet first with shining limbs, he glanced down from above among the bushes. . . . In the burning, intolerable sunlight he stood, and I in the shade of the bushes. . . . "Come out," he said with a taunt. "Art thou afraid to meet me?" And I answered not, but sprang upon him and smote him. And he smote me a thousand times, and lashed and scorched and slew me as with hands of flame; and I was glad, for my body lay there dead; and I sprang upon him again with another body; and he turned upon me, and smote me a thousand times and slew that body; and I was glad and sprang upon him again with another body. . . . And with another and another and again another; and the bodies which I took on yielded before him, and were like cinctures of flame upon me, but I flung them aside; and the pains which I endured in one body were powers which I wielded in the next; and I grew in strength till at last I stood before him complete, with a body like his own and equal in might—exultant in pride and joy. . . . Then he ceased and said: "I love thee." And lo! his form changed and he leaned backwards and drew me upon him. And he bore me up into the air and floated me over the topmost trees and the ocean and round the curve of the earth under the moon.... Till we stood again in Paradise'...

And this is how St. John in Revelation (ii.) sums up the whole matter: 'And he that *overcometh* and keepeth my works unto the end, to him will I give power over the nations.... And I will give him the *morning star*.'

. . . . .

The Illusion Called Evil

We have come to regard evil as an entity with intelligence of its own and this incorrect belief has led to much fear and misunderstanding. What is called evil is force or energy turned in the wrong direction. The energy itself is *neutral* and can be used by us in whichever direction our freewill dictates. As an example we can use atomic force to blow up a city or to provide it with illumination. The choice is ours. If the universal Primary Energy reached earth levels as pure Light, then our gift of freewill would be lost, because mankind would only then be able to follow the Light without any other choice. This Energy therefore reaches us in a completely *neutral* form, available for our individual use in any direction we desire, good, bad or indifferent.

If you or I determine to use this Energy for selfish or other wrong ends, in time we involuntarily infuse it with an intelligent 'life' of its own, whereupon it begins to dominate our thoughts and actions, until in extreme cases we appear to lose all freewill and so become the tool and not the master. When Jesus released the 'devils' from those who were obsessed, what He was doing was to bring the energy concerned back to 'neutral', depriving it of the 'intelligence' it had been given, hence ready again for proper usage. When Jesus said 'Get thee behind me Satan' He was referring to an embodiment of energy into which human misuse had infused a seeming maleficent life and intelligence of its own. The accumulation over the ages of wrong thinking and acting has resulted in creating temporarily a state of 'Hell' in the invisible realms around us.

· · · · ·

Some traditionalists tell us that every word in our Scriptures represents God's truth and nothing else. By 'Word' in this connection is meant the actual English words used in our translations of the Bible from Greek, Latin and Hebrew. They pin their complete faith to the Authorised, Revised or some modern English translation, thereby ignoring some very important considerations.

The many and varied interpretations placed on Jesus' words by listeners and translators has resulted in the fact that after passing through Greek and Latin forms our English embodiment of the ideas used by Jesus does not give a clear or accurate interpretation of what He actually said nearly two thousand years ago, whether He was speaking in Greek, Hebrew or Aramaic as the case may be. It is only by Divine Grace that we are in possession of His teaching in a form which does retain so much of truth and illumination. Jesus and other great teachers never regarded 'evil' as an intelligent and independent entity even if many of the sayings that have come down to us in garbled form seem to imply that this is so.

In a spiritual and only real sense evil (and all its works) is an illusion, resulting from the misuse of the imagination. 'That which I greatly feared has come upon me,' said Job. His fear was only a mental figment until he 'feared' it out into manifestation. On the practical plane, never speak or think of anyone as an 'evil man or woman' but recognise that the energy being used is directed by him in the wrong direction and that this process can and will be rectified, sooner or later through conscious reorientation of the force in question. Then the so-called evil disappears and in fact it never had anything but a transitory existence within the human mind. To impersonalise evil is to win half the battle in grappling with its pretensions to dominion over us. Evil is man-made, not God-created.

God created His Universe pure and perfect and behold all that He made was and is good. The Mystery of the Fall of Man into the worlds of unreality will become explained and understood so soon as we are ready for this revelation. When this happens it could well become the prelude to the return of the Golden Age and to the disappearance of all illusory states of life and being.

One final thought. The Creator's supreme gift to man is that of the capacity to receive and respond to the infinite Love of God. This gift ensures the ultimate salvation of humanity. Without it life itself would prove valueless and man's freewill would include the risk of his final destruction. But God who gave us the greatest gift of all can never deprive us of it. Our appreciation of this truth frees the mind from the almost intolerable burden of belief in original sin. Here and now and always let us take full advantage of our heritage of that Love which passeth understanding, one that will remain our most precious possession throughout eternity.

Chapter Eleven

Times of Tribulation

THERE IS CONFUSION of thought in many people's minds about the venue and significance of the final conflict of this age, often referred to as 'Armageddon' or the Times of Tribulation.

What is not generally realised is the fact that the main arena for this struggle between the forces of light and darkness is not situated in our outer world of life and being at all. Fundamentally, this great battle is being fought out on a different level and what we are experiencing on earth is a reflection of this immense struggle and the repercussions flowing from it. This does not mean that we play no part in what is going on 'elsewhere'. On the contrary, our every thought, word and deed can help to tip the scales in one direction or the other, because the battleground is on a mental level to which our thinking and feeling processes have access.

The means by which events taking place in invisible spheres around us throw their light and shadow into human consciousness and are translated into conditions directly affecting external happenings on our planet is not known to us. Study of the interplay of forces between various levels of life and being belongs to the science of the future. What we cannot doubt is that under Divine Providence the law of cause and effect operates justly, and has always done so, not only in the affairs of men and of nations but in relation to all manifestation of life everywhere, and that this law is based on infinite love in action.

It is, I think, true of the human race as a whole as it is of single individuals that no one can live unto himself alone. In fact, I feel that this principle is capable of a still wider and deeper application covering experiences and events taking place far beyond the time-space conditions within which we are confined at present.

The long-standing interior struggle between Light and Darkness, what we call 'good' and 'evil', is as old as time. It now appears to be reaching its culmination for the particular era to which we belong. This is almost certainly the 'Armageddon' forecast in Scriptures to take place 'at the end of the age'. Its *reflection* on this planet, in so far as space-time conditions are concerned, appears to have been in operation since 1914 and will probably last for about half a century. History will no doubt record three acute phases of this manifestation, represented by the 1914-1918 and 1939-1945 wars, and by what we hope will be a comparatively short period from 1958 onwards, the third phase being the most critical and the most decisive. However, the reflection in our world of events happening elsewhere cannot be accurately interpreted or measured by finite sense. The point I should like to make is that the process of 'Armageddon' as reflected in our world is not still in the future, as many people imagine, but has been going on since at least 1914, and that its final repercussions affecting life on earth will depend upon who will be the victors in the invisible struggle between Light and Darkness referred to above, and also upon our human reactions both to the struggle itself and to the victory.

If this be a correct assessment of the position, we should ask ourselves what we can do as individuals in humble service to God and to those great Beings who direct the battalions of the Light. There is a certain sense in which the whole universe is contained within each one of us. And it is this universe for which each individual is responsible. The area for *our* battle between the light and dark forces lies within your consciousness and mine, because this battle is personal to you and to me. We can live in such a way as to be capable of reflecting and declaring the power of the Light out into manifestation, or we can allow the dark forces of our natures to secure the upper hand. There can be no neutrals in this struggle. You and I are personally responsible for the outcome of this 'Armageddon of the Soul'. It is beyond our finite understanding to compute the extent to which our thoughts and acts can influence the struggle as a whole. However, this much we can know: namely, that it lies within your and my power by our prayers, thoughts and actions to reinforce the armies of the Light and to an extent which, cumulatively, may well prove decisive. Or we can provide ammunition for the dark forces by selfish preoccupation with our own desires, ambitions and sensuous pleasures, thereby giving the Light no opportunity to be reflected and manifested through us and, as a direct result, intensifying the agony of the conflict. Each one, therefore, can play his part in prolonging the time of tribulation or in shortening it.

Until the present epic struggle 'in high places' has been fought out and, as we must firmly believe, won by the Powers of the Light, and until this victory has been reflected in human consciousness, there can be no return of the Christ among us, nor can the Golden Age be born. There is a certain sense in which the Christ, as the supreme representative of the Creator, is never absent from the hearts and minds of men (that is, to the extent to which we are willing to receive Him). But His *active* manifestation in our midst once more must inevitably depend upon our willingness to create the right conditions for such a manifestation to take place successfully. It cannot be His function to interfere with the working of the law of cause and effect.

I should like to pause here a moment to speak about the event scripturally referred to as the 'Day of Judgment'. Each time we pass from one level of life to another we shall find ourselves faced by a 'Day of Judgment' when the accounts will be reckoned and when whatever debit balance stands against us will have to be met and paid. This is a truth which I think is recognised in the teaching of all religions.

Whether there is to be a *final* 'day' of reckoning for humanity as a whole and for individual men and women is a question that lies far beyond our present knowledge. What does seem probable is that 'Days of Judgment' occur periodically not only in our own lives but also in the life of nations and peoples and planets. Our knowledge of human history does not go back very far. For instance, accounts of the 'Flood' and of the disappearance of Atlantis and Lemuria have come down to us in a legendary form only. Is it inconceivable that such happenings have a direct relation to the subject we are discussing? It may be that from time to time in world history the accumulation of wrong thinking and acting becomes so burdensome in its effects that a drastic cleansing process proves inevitable, providing the opportunity for a wiping of the slate and the provision of a clean surface in order to make a fresh start possible. We may not be far distant from such happenings as have just been mentioned.

In this connection one is reminded of the words of Bossuet:

Quand Dieu éfface, c'est qu'Il se prépare à écrire.

In giving consideration to the ideas I have expressed, it may be helpful to remember that whatever may seem to be happening in the illusory worlds around us, *'the Government is upon His shoulders'*. It is within our power to receive the protection of this Government and to take our modest part in carrying out its laws and dictates.

As events unroll, it may be only too easy to give entry into our minds to the two great enemies: Fear and Depression. Bar the gates against them! On the other hand, welcome into the home of your spirit, Faith, Serenity and Courage. Open your doors widely to receive and entertain these three good friends, and be at peace.

Realise that the sun never ceases to shine; however dark the clouds may be which seem to obscure its light, these clouds are temporary, in relation to eternity, and possess no real substance. For this good reason . . . let us give thanks!

CHAPTER TWELVE

A Colloquy Between the Author and his Publisher

HAVING READ THROUGH a portion of the scripts which are now included in this book, my publisher approached me and in a most courteous manner made the following request.

He enquired whether I would be willing to comment on certain subjects dealt with which he felt needed some elucidation. I was not in the least surprised, being fully aware that for many readers much that I have written will be perplexing to them. This is not altogether my fault. The language of the words at present available is totally inadequate to explain many of the conceptions which I have been trying to outline. Our present vocabulary is at best a feeble vehicle for expressing ideas and for describing conditions that lie outside the range of our material surroundings. However, I suggested that if a short questionnaire might be prepared I would do my best to comment upon its contents. This questionnaire duly arrived, so let us get to work upon it.

Question A. How can you expect anyone to believe anything you say without concrete evidence of its truth?

W. T. P.: I have no expectations. As has been said earlier in these notes, it is not feasible to produce what is called 'concrete evidence' in support of the interior experiences of the mind. Even if one could, there is little reason to suppose that those to whom such experiences are foreign would be convinced. When predictions concerning future events are published before such events happen, and if such predictions prove correct, the evidence is there, but even then it is often regarded as resulting from coincidence.

A more pertinent query is as follows: We come into this world presumably to make the best use possible of the conditions we find here. Surely it is unwise to allow our thoughts and actions to be diverted towards the study of 'other-worldly' states and conditions? My first comment would be to suggest that we are here not only to make the best use of the conditions we are born into, but to seek to improve upon them. If the study of metaphysics can help in this connection, so much the better. I agree with the questioner's inference that there may be danger of such study distracting us unduly from our day-to-day duties and responsibilities. Unless one's feet are firmly planted on the ground and the reasoning faculty is kept alert, experiences of a supernatural order may well upset the balance of our lives. Certainly indulgence in artificial methods for the purpose of trying to widen our range of knowledge is to be avoided. Until the race emerges from adolescence it would be dangerous for the veil to be removed entirely which now separates our world of thought and being from the wider realms of consciousness into which we pass at 'death'.

Having said this, there is I feel still something further to be remembered. Both world and personal problems are beyond solution if we rely solely upon the power of the human mind unaided to solve them. The pride of the intellect refuses to believe this, and especially so is this the case in social, scientific and political circles. If therefore there be those among us who are suitably equipped for exploring regions which lie at present beyond our normal ken, surely in the common interest they should be encouraged to do so? To reject out of hand the experience of such explorers, because of the transcendental nature of their findings, is I feel to be deplored.

There are dangers inherent in every form of research into the unknown, and those dangers should be recognised and safeguarded against: nevertheless, the exploration should go on.

It is often argued that interest in these matters is morbid and unnatural. If, however, it be true, as my own researches tend to suggest, that we on earth are subject to unseen influences and energies, whether we be conscious of the fact or not, then the exploration of these 'borderland' conditions is of importance to us here and now. Some day no doubt such research will be developed into a science and many cosmic laws, at present unknown and unrecognised, will be tabulated for our guidance and our safety. Meanwhile, pioneers in this field should not be perturbed unduly by criticism and misunderstanding of their aims and motives.

There is one direction in particular where modern civilisation has fallen into grievous error. The value of silence and the training of the mind to become still and receptive has ceased to be recognised and practised. We educate our children almost entirely through the use of noise. They are taught to focus their attention upon what they hear and see. In their homes and at school they are surrounded by continual clamour, to which are now added the mechanical distractions of radio and television and the roads.

The immense importance of silence as an integral part of education is rarely recognised. Training in the stilling of the mind, in thought control, is never given and the results are serious. The practice of silence can become a healing and educative agency, and it is time that this truth should be recognised and made available, both for children and adults alike. Even such a simple practice as the keeping of a Silent Minute each day is a step in the right direction. The Quakers and many Eastern sects draw much of their strength and inspiration from that deep interior silence which brings inspiration and peace.

Question B: In these 'latter days' are there people who have evolved beyond the present evolution incarnated on this planet, and who have returned to guide us within the limits to which they are permitted by Karmic or universal law?

W. T. P.: Yes, there are reasons for believing that this is so. The fact that the presence of such highly evolved beings in our midst is not generally recognised need not cause undue anxiety. They work silently, powerfully and with set purpose. They are imbued with a selfless love of humanity far beyond anything that we can conceive. I cannot go further into this very important subject just now. The time is not ripe.

Question C: In regard to the Second Coming, could it be possible that the disciples who were with Our Lord two thousand years ago will be with Him again when He returns, and perhaps indeed have already incarnated to prepare the way?

W. T. P.: Use of the term 'Second Coming' is liable to give a wrong impression of an event about which much confusion persists. The eternal Christ of God is not a being Who 'comes and goes' or passes from one level of life and being to another in endless succession. In this sense the 'Christ' is ever present everywhere and we can each recognise and receive this Presence if we will. Or we can reject it. The Spirit of Christ manifested in a supreme way through Jesus during the Master's years of ministry on earth. The same Spirit, in various manners and degrees, manifests through great spiritual masters and initiates at all times throughout human history and has never ceased to do so. It can manifest through you and through me to the extent that we are able to become dedicated channels for the purpose. When the need arises and the 'call' is strong enough, the same Christ selects the body of a dedicated 'master' through whom to give forth a message for the enlightenment of man, and especially so at the beginning of each new 'age' as the evolution of life on this planet proceeds.

The expectation that such an event may be imminent now is widespread, both within the world's great faiths and outside them. Seers can tell us that 'Preparers of the Way' for such a coming are already in our midst. It may well be that many 'dedicated disciples' from the past are among them. I have dealt more fully with this important subject elsewhere.

Question D: As earth moves into the Aquarian Age, what specific differences will we notice? Will, for instance, the vibrationary tempo change?

W. T. P.: A gradual quickening of men's perceptive faculty is already in evidence and this is not confined to members of any one creed, class or race. The use of the term you refer to as 'vibrationary tempo' may cause confusion because the word 'vibration' is often applied solely to the electrical and allied material fields of operation.

The rhythm of life and thought is already beginning to be attuned to a new keynote, suitable for use during the coming dispensation. Here again the subject is too vast to be dealt with in a casual note like this.

However, as a hint to help the discerning seeker, this can be disclosed. A quality of Deity hitherto not available to men on earth is now beginning to unfold. This quality or attribute could be referred to symbolically as a Blended Ray, the child of the union of Love and Wisdom. This ray will produce a new rhythm within human consciousness and it is within this rhythm that the message for the coming age will manifest. No word has yet been coined to describe this new quality or to define its attributes or effects. The word 'new' in this connection only refers to the fact that the newness applies to human consciousness now for the first time, in so far as evolution on this planet is concerned. The keynote for this quality will be sounded in a very special way, by the Christ messenger now believed to be approaching our level of existence.

Question E: It is understood that many people all over the world are coming together in groups, big and small, to learn how to adjust themselves to the new Aquarian Age which we are said to have already entered. Could the Blended Ray have a harmful effect on some of these groups if they are not under proper guidance and leadership? Are there evolved souls in sufficient numbers on this planet—people capable of functioning harmoniously in such a high state of consciousness and rhythm—who will be able themselves to act as 'lighthouses' and diffuse the light to those who are seeking, but are perhaps less evolved and trained occultly than themselves? This seems of importance, as it has been said that too much light can blind those not accustomed to it.

W. T. P.: The Blended Ray will undoubtedly possess a cleansing and harmonising influence within human consciousness and it will bring with it a new vista of revelation for mankind. The cleansing process may prove drastic and testing but its effects will certainly not be harmful or depressive. It is true that the responsibilities of those who act as leaders in every field of human activity will be greater and more far-reaching than at any previous period in the evolution of the race. Nevertheless as I have said before, revelation is an interior and personal experience and as a consequence each individual should look for spiritual guidance from within rather than from without.

If a sufficient number of men and women of the will-to-good in every walk of life can be found (and their number is steadily increasing) then the 'lighthouses' to which you refer will prove adequate and their number and influence will grow in proportion to the awakened demand that is made upon them.

To use an electrical analogy, there will become available for human service many initiates, seers and 'elder brothers' active both in bodily form and otherwise whose mission will be to act as 'transformers'.

Many of us who cannot claim to be in the above categories are already acting in this way and in a certain sense the contents of books like this can be regarded as transforming agencies. The cosmic energy behind the Blended Ray will not be allowed to defeat its own purposes, even if to the casual onlooker it may appear as if shock tactics were in operation, designed to arouse the sleeper and to carry out the task of opening closed minds and hearts.

In this respect there will be found suggestions in the notes in 'Times of Tribulation' which may help to bring a measure of understanding.

The ultimate direction and control of the Blended Ray belongs to One who will manifest the Christ for the New Age. That great being known to us as Michael the Archangel* and his Messengers are the 'Preparers of the Way' and we can each do our part to help them in their present mission. Michael can in fact be regarded not only as the eternal standard-bearer for the Christ, but as the transformer-in-chief of the energies of the Blended Ray which is now approaching.

Question F: Can you explain the difference between negative and positive thought? Would a third world war provide more negative thought and a cosmic upheaval which we might well be powerless to halt and so destroy the earth through cataclysms?

---

* *Michael Prince of Heaven* (J. M. Watkins, London).

W. T. P.: 'Negative' and 'positive' are relative terms. What to some of us may seem to be negative thinking may well be the closest approach to positive thinking that those concerned can reach, at the point of evolution where they now stand. Wars and all happenings in our midst of what we call a 'disastrous' kind produce both negative and positive thought and action. In another context, a mental attitude that is attuned to fear, depression, anxiety, will by its very incidence attract more negative and devolutionary influences. An attitude of mind attuned to the principles of love, service and selflessness will, on the other hand, create the right conditions for progress and upliftment. Dwelling upon the fear of cataclysms, a third world war and similar disasters, can do immense harm, tending to create the very conditions suitable for such events to happen.

Question G: How can prayer help the individual and produce cosmic changes and positive results?

W. T. P.: Dr. Alexis Carrel has wisely stated that 'prayer is the inexhaustible motive power that spins the universe'. A conscious turning towards God through prayer and meditation opens the gates through which illumination and wisdom can flow into human consciousness. This form of prayer is selfless, not being concerned with asking the Deity to satisfy our immediate personal and mundane needs. The prayer of affirmation of all that is in accordance with love and beauty, of the power of light over darkness, such prayer is the best means for combating the effects of negative thought and action. Each of us is a universe within himself, and if we think and do the best we know, within this universe, then we are helping to create a leaven within human consciousness as a whole.

Question H: Can you explain time and space in connection with cosmic laws and why we ought to get outside time and space in our thinking and actions? In other words, try to reach out into a fourth dimension.

W. T. P.: No short answer to this question would prove of real value. We are capable here and now of using the faculties of our minds to operate beyond and outside what you refer to as 'time-space' conditions. Many of the experiences related in this book indicate how the mind can function outside time and space and quite apart from the use of the brain, the latter being unable to register clearly experiences that take place outside the regions governed by time and space. The mind of man is not confined in its activities to three dimensions, even if the brain would try to affirm that this is so.

When you or I endeavour to lift up our eyes and our minds to the hills, to become receptive to the light of inspiration ever waiting for our acceptance and use, we are active in 'dimensions' which far transcend the three dimensions of time, space and form (matter).

No words are available to explain the working of cosmic laws. Revelation in this field can only come to you and to me as a spiritual and interior experience.

Question I: In your description of a visit to the house in Jerusalem where the Last Supper was held as related in *The Upper Room* you speak of the use of two faculties of the mind referred to as the participant and the observer. Was this experience recorded as the result of a memory of actual events?*

W. T. P.: In my note on the elasticity of time in 'Memory, Time and Prevision' I have tried to deal with some aspects of this problem. Although the incidents referred to appeared to be taking place at the very moment when the experience came to me in A.D. 1959, with myself both as participant and observer, it seems reasonable to believe that, through the use of memory, I was reliving through events which actually took place just before the period of the Crucifixion in the first century A.D.

Some readers may be inclined to think that I was

* See Part 2, Chapter 6.

recollecting the details of events with which I had been associated during a previous life on earth. There could be other explanations, too complex to deal with in this note. On a future occasion and after further research I shall hope to pursue this investigation further.

Question J: What effect is the emergence of the Blended Ray likely to have on orthodox religion?

W. T. P.: The wind of the Spirit bloweth where it listeth. Its breath will be felt within palaces, prisons and in the humblest homes. This fresh outpouring of energy to which I have referred as the Blended Ray will permeate churches, synagogues, mosques and temples. No human barriers will be able to keep it out or to withstand its presence for very long. The fermentation already so apparent within religious organisations is a presage of events to come. The time is not yet when man will be sufficiently mature to dispense altogether with form and ceremonies and the use of ritual. 'The Church' referred to by the Master Jesus is awaiting to be discerned within the sanctuary of the soul.

Meanwhile there is hope that the churches and temples of every faith will begin to adapt their institutions to meet the current needs of man as he journeys forward on his pilgimage towards the light. The breaking of old bottles and the fashioning of new ones is a process that has never ceased to operate and will continue to do so throughout human history.

It can be a painful process, as indeed it is today, a cause of bewilderment and distress to many people, including those who practise their religion and those who call themselves materialists.

· · · · ·

There are signs around us today which suggest that the gap between science and religion is in process of being bridged. I believe this to be true in spite of the fact that some famous exponents of modern science continue to assert that religion in all its forms has no impact on the evolution of the human race and is therefore valueless. The physicist has now traced matter back to its point of origin namely, force or energy. The next step forward will be to discover the source of this energy and its causation. Even the conception and the working of a mechanistic universe would be inconceivable without the services of a Master Mechanic. I predict that before the present century has run its course, discoveries in science and metaphysics will have shaken the standpoint of the materialist to its foundations, thereby rendering his position quite untenable.

Discovery and revelation are twins that should not be rent apart, the one working from below, the other from above. As we enter the age now dawning it will be the activities of the Blended Ray under Divine direction that will merge the two in a manner of inestimable benefit to all mankind. Each one of us, in ways too numerous to calculate, can be instruments through the service of humanity as a whole.

One final thought—man's discoveries in all fields of research can prove very dangerous to him unless accompanied by the revelation of how such discoveries should be harnessed and put to uses that are both right and good. In other words, the discoveries of material science, through the use of reason from without and revelation through the exercise of intuition from within, must be united once and for all and never allowed to become separated again.

CHAPTER THIRTEEN

Chalice Well and 'The Upper Room'

AT THE BEGINNING of 1959 it was my privilege to launch a wonderful adventure. The Chalice Well estate at Glastonbury, Somerset, lies on the slopes of Chalice Hill, almost under the shadow of the far-famed Michael Tor. For centuries past this hallowed site had been in private ownership, not easy of access to visitors and pilgrims.

With the co-operation of a group of friends, the property has now been vested in a charitable trust and the hallowed well, the gardens and Little St. Michael Hostel are now open to all comers, irrespective of race, class or creed. History, legend and tradition surround this site, being intermingled in a way that is both mysterious and perhaps unique. This is not the place to review in detail a past which stretches across two thousand years and more.

The story has already been told in many books and pamphlets readily available to all who are interested in Celtic Christianity and the arrival of Christ's Message in Britain within fifty years of the Crucifixion. Earlier in this book I have touched upon the mystery of premonition. Here is a case in point. I visited Glastonbury and Chalice Well for the first time in 1904 and at a time when the Chalice Well property belonged to a Catholic Order. I was allowed to visit the well and to drink the healing and vitalising waters from its spring. I was also permitted to roam over the gardens surrounding it and to spend some time in the adjoining orchard which lies farther up the slopes of Chalice Hill. I was left with a feeling of sanctity and inspiration, which has never left me. And I was left with something more, namely the premonition that in time to come I should be given the opportunity to come into the possession of this truly wonderful place, so that it might be thrown open to all who believe in the Brotherhood of Man under the Fatherhood of God. Over half a century was to pass before the event fulfilled the premonition. Strange are the ways of Destiny!

One of the legends closely associated with Chalice Well has lived on since early Christian times and has refused to die or to be forgotten. It tells of the arrival of Joseph of Arimathea (reputed to have been the uncle on his mother's side of Our Lord) at Chalice Well some years after the Ascension. He came, it is said, with a devoted group of disciples, to bring Christ's message to our country and to settle here.

Joseph is believed to have brought with him the Cup used at the Last Supper and to have buried it for safe keeping beneath Chalice Hill within a stone's throw of the well itself. One of the first books published by the Chalice Well Trust is called *The Upper Room*. This contains what purports to be a description of the Master's Cup, which in medieval times came to be linked in men's hearts and minds with the lovely mysticism of the Holy Grail.

The message carried by this little book has already brought response from readers scattered right across the world. I am happy to have this opportunity of thanking all those who have written me about it, as the letters received are far too numerous to reply to individually.

I believe that the Cup or Chalice is destined to become the symbol for the new age now dawning, and it is my hope that Chalice Well may once more fulfil the inspiring mission of acting as a gateway through which revelation for coming times may flow, radiating from there across Britain and the world.

It is my conviction that the people of our Island will be given the opportunity once more to lead humanity out of its present darkness into the Light.

The beams from the Lighthouse which is within our power to build may well be destined to radiate Illumination to the far corners of the Earth.

I firmly believe that it lies within the capacity of our children and their children to carry out this task. In my view the discerning among them should lose no time in preparing themselves to fulfil a Destiny that most surely will be presented to them and at no very distant date.

Readers who are interested can obtain further information from the Custodian, Chalice Well Trust, Little St. Michael, Glastonbury, Somerset.